1.77

PREACHING VALUES
FROM THE PAPYRI

PREACHING VALUES
FROM THE PAPYRI

by

HERSCHEL H. HOBBS

BAKER BOOK HOUSE
Grand Rapids, Michigan
1964

PHOTOLITHOPRINTED BY CUSHING - MALLOY, INC.
ANN ARBOR, MICHIGAN, UNITED STATES OF AMERICA
1964

DEDICATION
to
WILLIAM HERSEY DAVIS
who first introduced me to the study of the
Greek Papyri, and led me to appreciate its
value in interpreting the New Testament.

INTRODUCTION

What did the message contained in the New Testament mean to the generation which first heard and/or read it? Would the answer to this question enhance our own understanding of the gospel? Should these questions be of interest to a twentieth-century preacher of the gospel? The author's conviction that these questions call for affirmative answers is the basis of this volume.

The New Testament was written in *KOINĒ* Greek, a shortened form of *hē koinē dialektē*, "the common tongue" or dialect. Students of the language know that it differs from Classical Greek. Through the years it was called "New Testament Greek," as though it were a language prepared especially for the writing of the New Testament. One German scholar, R. Rothe, called it "a languauge of the Holy Ghost."

But the discovery of Greek papyri has changed this concept of the language used in the New Testament. On this material (papyri) were written such everyday items as official documents, tax and census records, marriage and divorce contracts, notices of birth and death, grocery bills, and private letters. Naturally these were written, not in the language of classical scholars, but in that of the common people.

It was Doctor Adolf Deissmann who discovered the similarity between the language of the papyri and that of the New Testament. Thus the latter is not "a language of the Holy Ghost." It was the language of the everyday communication of the people. Therefore, this discovery has thrown a flood of light on the meaning of the New Testament. There are less than fifty words found in the New Testament that are not found in the papyri or other current writings.

Words are pictures of ideas. A given word will contain many pictures. So when the first century people heard or read a certain Greek word it portrayed many meanings. This means that a given word often was much richer in meaning than that which came down to us by way of stated theological vocabulary.

The purpose of this volume is to study a selected group of Greek words found in the New Testament. The procedure is to examine a word as it appears in the papyri and in the New Testament, seeking to point out any enrichment derived from the former with respect to the interpretation of the latter.

Hence the title *Preaching Values from the Papyri.* If this volume serves to enrich one sermon by one preacher it will have accomplished the purpose for which it is written.

But it is the author's hope that the use of this volume will not be confined to preachers alone. The very nature of this work makes it necessary that we approach it from the stand-point of the original language of the papyri and of the New Testament. Copious examples of the Greek words are included with the hope that this will enrich its meaning for those who are versed in the Greek language. But along with this the English translations are included, thus making their value available to all other students, preachers, and teachers of the New Testament. With rare exceptions no attempt is made to give either the dates or the original language of the papyri examples. The important thing is to give the English transla-tions of these examples and to relate them to the New Testa-ment passages where these words are used. Exact dates of the examples are not of primary importance for this work. They range all the way from the third century B.C. to the fourth century A.D. But their usage serves to show the current mean-ing of given words in the period just prior to, during, and immediately after the time of the writing of the New Testa-ment. And since in most instances these meanings span the years, in some cases carrying over into Modern Greek, they are of value to show their connotations in the New Testament itself.

Basic in this study is the large volume *The Vocabulary of the Greek New Testament* by James Hope Moulton and George Milligan (Eerdmans Publishing Company, Grand

Rapids, Michigan, 1949). References to A. T. Robertson are from his *Word Pictures of the New Testament* (Sunday School Board of the Southern Baptist Convention, Nashville, 1930). An occasional reference is made to *The Expositor's Greek Testament* (Eerdmans, Grand Rapids, 1951). Much valuable help is derived from *A Greek-English Lexicon of the New Testament*, an English translation by W. F. Ardnt and F. W. Gingrich of W. Bauer's German volume, published by The University of Chicago Press, 1957. This is one of the most accurate Greek lexicons since it makes wide use of the papyri. References to Thayer are from his *Greek-English Lexicon of the New Testament* (American Book Company, 1886), a standard work but which by necessity of its date makes no use of the papyri.

Herschel H. Hobbs

First Baptist Church
Oklahoma City, Oklahoma
October 7, 1963

CONTENTS

AIRŌ

(Away with Him!)

This verb is found often in the New Testament (102 times). It means variously to take, take up, take away, lift up or to bear. In Matthew 27:32 it is used of Simon of Cyrene bearing the cross of Jesus (bearing something not his own for another, cf. John 1:29).

While there are a number of examples of this word found in the papyri, only three instances throw any particular light on its use in the New Testament. One such is a command. "Take those things out of the midst" or way *(aron tauta ek tou mesou)*. This is almost an exact parallel to Colossians 2:14, ". . . and took it out of the way . . ." *(ērken ek tou mesou)*. Although this papyri example comes in the second/third century A.D. it shows a similarity of expression with Paul's famous phrase.

Another deals with the payment allotted to the *bearers* *(ērkasi)* of a corpse. This is slightly suggestive of John 1:29, "Behold the Lamb of God which taketh away the sin of the world." As the Lamb of God, Jesus in His death takes away the corpse of sin, our death, from our lives.

But the most suggestive use is found in a mother's complaint about her son. "He upsets me: away with him" *(arron auton)*. This latter was almost the exact cry of the Jews against Jesus. "Away with him, away with him, crucify him" *(aron aron, stauróson auton)* (John 19:14; cf. Luke 23:18; Acts 21:36; 22:22). It is because Jesus *upsets* us that we nail Him to the cross in our sinful lives.

AGŌN, AGŌNIA, AGŌNIZOMAI

(Fightings Within, Without)

These words form a family of words used variously of athletic contests or of warfare. *Agōn* referred to both the contest and the place where it was held. From *agōnia* comes our word "agony." It connotes a violent struggle. *Agōnizomai* is the verb form meaning to be a participant in such. In studying these words it is well to look also at *gumnazō* (treated later in this volume). It speaks of training in the gymnasium for the contest. The present words under study deal with the contest itself, either athletic or military.

Moulton and Milligan cite no papyri example of *agōnizomai*. But it abounds in the inscriptions in the sense of both warfare and striving in athletic contests.

However, several papyri usages of *agōn* are found. One such speaks of "the conflict of the soul." An example in 5 B.C. speaks of an agonizing effort to compel one to restore a stolen daughter. Another expresses the great effort in the discipline of a child. This word is also used of the games at Oxyrhynchus, a usage which is most relevant to Hebrews 12:1. Plutarch (not papyri) says, "But he had much greater difficulties to combat, when he applied to Manius in behalf of the Chalcidians." Thus we see the ethical sense of mental and spiritual combat, as well as that found in athletic contests.

The use of *agōnia* abounds in the papyri. Sometimes it is used in the sense of great anxiety: "So I am at present very anxious"; "For we are in a state of no ordinary anxiety." It is rendered as "worry." One example reads, "Do not worry" (*mē agōniais*). Another: "I urge you therefore not to worry."

12

These examples serve to show the multiple use of these words. But always in the background is the basic idea of a great struggle as seen in warfare or in athletic contests. This will prove helpful as we examine their use in the New Testament.

The verb *agōnizomai* is found seven times in the New Testament (Luke 13:24; John 18:36; I Cor. 9:25; Col. 1:29; 4:12; I Tim. 6:12; II Tim. 4:7). In Luke 13:24 Jesus says, "Strive to enter in at the strait gate. . . ." This suggests the extreme difficulty of doing so. In fact "strive" *(agonizesthe)* may best be understood if we imagine the rigorous training required of a successful athlete. Better still, if we imagine soldiers in warfare storming the gates of a city. The military aspect of this word is clearly seen in John 18:36. ". . .if my kingdom were of this world then would my servants fight [*ēgōnizonto*] that I should not be delivered to the Jews. . . ."

The remaining examples of the verb are in the writings of Paul who was fond of drawing upon both athletic and military terms to express spiritual truth.

One of his most striking figures drawn from athletics is found in I Corinthians 9:24-27. He begins with a reference to the races in which only one receives the prize of victory (v. 24). And then he adds the figure of boxing (v. 26). In verse 25 he says, "And every man that striveth [*agōnizomenos*, the one striving in the game] is temperate in all things." Contestants were subjected to a rigorous period of training (ten months) under trained coaches, during which they had no wine and ate a very strict diet. This, Paul says, they did for a corruptible crown of victory, usually made of parsley or pine leaves (Isthmian games), or olive leaves (Olymphian games) This soon faded away. Paul and all Christians strive for an incorruptible crown.

Therefore, he says that he runs, "not uncertainly." He knows his goal, Christ. He fights (*pukteuō*, from which comes our word *pugilist*) "not as one who beats the air" (v. 26). He is no *shadow boxer*. A pugilist shadow boxes at times while in training for a fight. When he enters the ring he has a real opponent. Paul says that he is really in the fight. And he is

fighting to win. In verse 27 he reveals that he himself, or his
physical body, is his opponent. "Keep my body under" means
"I buffet my body." "Buffet" (*hupōpiazō*, from *hupo* and *ops*,
the part of the face under the eyes) means a blow on that
part of the face. A. T. Robertson suggests the rendering, "I
beat my body black and blue."

And Paul does this that he might not "be a castaway."
Literally, "I myself be rejected." This does not mean that he
would not be saved. He had to be a *Christian* to be in these
games. The point is that he wants to win the prize (cf. v. 24).
He wants to excel all others in these spiritual games, games
which are made all the more meaningful because of the application of current terminology to Christian truth.

In Colossians 4:12 Paul applies this same idea of *striving*
to prayer. Epaphras was "always laboring fervently" (*pantote
agōnizomenos*) for the Colossian Christians "in prayers." He
wrestles or fights in prayer on their behalf. Thus prayer is
the spiritual weapon to ward off the evil one and his designs.

The remainder of Paul's usages of *agōnizomai* are used in
combination with *agōn*, which serves to intensify the meaning
of both. For instance, note Colossians 1:29—2:1. That he
"may present every man perfect [complete] in Christ" (v. 28),
he labors, "striving [*agōnizomenos*] according to his working
[energy], the one energizing in me in power" (v. 29, author's
translation). Paul's conflict on their behalf is in the *energy*
of Christ in him. This passage is enhanced in meaning when
we interpret it in the light of the dual meaning of *agōnizomai* (athletic and military) in the papyri.

In Colossians 2:1 Paul uses the word *agōn*, "conflict." Some
see this as spiritual conflict. Others regard it as actual combat.
But there is no record of such. In all probability the apostle
is drawing on the military sense of the word to express the
spiritual warfare which he wages on their behalf. For a full
treatment of this idea throughout Colossians, see my *Christ
In You* (Baker Book House, 1961).

A most interesting combination of these two words is found
in I Timothy 6:12, where Paul exhorts Timothy to "*fight* the
good *fight* of faith" (author's italics). Note the verb and noun

respectively. Either the athletic or military sense fits here. Another such example is seen in II Timothy 4:7. "I *have fought* a good *fight*. . ." (author's italics). At this point this could be either athletic or military. But that Paul here is thinking of a race is seen in the words "finished my course" and "crown of righteousness" (v. 8). A "course" (*dromos*) was the race track. The "crown" is the victor's crown bestowed at such races. But note that when we compare this with I Corinthians 9:24ff. either a boxing match or a race could be applied. At any rate Paul has gained that for which he was *agonizing*. He has won the prize. He is not a "castaway." He did not come out second-best in the contest.

Further uses of *agōn* are found in Philippians 1:30; I Thessalonians 2:2; and Hebrews 12:1. In Philippians 1:30 Paul speaks of his "conflict" (*agōn*) as his sufferings for Christ. I Thessalonians 2:2 renders this word "contention." The word "conflict" fits better. Paul reminds the Thessalonian Christians of the struggle which he had there in preaching the gospel to them. Some see this as inward or soul conflict. But it also refers to the outward conflict which he experienced there (cf. Acts 17:1-9).

In Hebrews 12:1 *agōn* is translated "race." This is in keeping with the papyri examples which use this word to refer to the Oxyrhynchus games. This is a most vivid picture. It probably refers to a relay race. The running of those who went before will not win the race (God's redemptive purpose for all men) unless each generation of God's people runs its part of the relay race faithfully (cf. 11:40, note "perfect," complete or successful). The "cloud of witnesses" are those who have successfully completed their part of the race, including Jesus, and are now watching as these Hebrew Christians ran theirs (12:1). Note the idea of an arena, an amphitheatre with tiers of seats filled with whose who have *witnessed*, not mere spectators.

"Weight" refers to the custom of Greek runners training with weights on their feet (weighted shoes are still used by some). They took them off to run. Thus they could run faster. The "easily besetting sin" suggests long clothes that would entangle their legs. Greek runners ran in the races almost naked. "Laying aside" refers to both the weights and the garments. Runners did not perform for the plaudits of the crowds, but for the favorable decision of the judges. Hence, "looking unto Jesus. . . ." He has been a fellow-participant (cf. "partakers," partners, Heb. 2:1), and is now the Judge.

Only one example of *agōnia* is found in the New Testament (Luke 22:44). It speaks of Jesus' "agony" in the Garden of Gethsemane. This is a most meaningful usage. However, we see more than *anxiety* or *worry* as found in the papyri examples.

In this usage we see all of the conflict and striving bound up in the basic meaning of the word. In fact, this would seem to carry the meaning of warfare. Jesus fought against Satan and all of his angels as He did battle for the will of God and for the souls of men. This is particularly seen in Luke's picture of "sweat . . . as it were great drops of blood." "Great drops of blood" could be either flowing or clotted blood. Both probably were true here. In this terminology we see Luke the Physician. For this is a term found in many Greek medical writings. A. T. Robertson notes that both Aristotle and Theophrastus speak of "a bloody sweat." So in this word *agōnia* we see the bloody Warrior bleeding from many wounds sustained as He waged war with the adversary of both God and man.

"But thanks be to God, which giveth us the victory through our Lord Jesus Christ!" (I Cor. 15:57) .

AKRATOS

(Untempered with Mercy)

This word is found only one time in the New Testament (Rev. 14:10). In classic Greek it means "unmixed" as of wine being unmixed with other substances. Modern Greek renders it "undiluted" as of milk. These meanings are in harmony with the reference in Revelation which speaks of "wine . . . without mixture."

However there is one example of *akratos* found in the papyri which adds even more to the usage in Revelation. In the legal sense it appears in the statement "amongst whom the severity of the law is untempered" *(akratos).*

Revelation 14:10 speaks of the wrath of God against those who worship the "beast and his image" (Roman Empire and emperor worship?). Two words are rendered "wrath." The former is *thumos,* or wrath expressed in passion, one which boils up but soon subsides (Thayer). The latter is *orgē,* or wrath which has arisen gradually and become more settled (Thayer). This is God's abiding opposition to sin which on occasion boils up in a passionate expression of anger *(thumos).* Thus out of the stored-up wrath of God's abiding indignation this passionate rage is poured. Revelation sees this as wine drawn from the "cup" or storage place of the stored-up wrath.

In this light a literal translation of Revelation 14:10 is most revealing. "And the same [those who worship the beast and his image] shall drink out of the wine of the passionate rage of God, of the one which has been prepared for drinking untempered [*akratos*] in the cup of his stored-up wrath . . . ." The words "poured out" (KJV) render a word meaning "to prepare for drinking." Literally this word followed by *akratos* means "the mixed unmixed" (Robertson). Thus the abiding wrath of God against sin which has been stored-up throughout the ages will suddenly burst forth in a passionate rage. It will be wrath "untempered" with mercy.

It was from this same "cup" *(potērion)* that Jesus drank on the cross (cf. John 18:11). For that reason all who believe in Him as Saviour will never drink of the "untempered" wrath of God.

APECHŌ

(Closing Out an Account)

This is a compound verb composed of *apo,* from or away from, and *echō,* I have, hold in the hands, or possess. It is used in both the New Testament and the papyri to denote distance or to be away from a place (cf. Matt. 15:8; Mark 7:6; Luke 7:6; 15:20; 24:13). However, this word has a far more picturesque usage in the papyri which throws much light on its meaning in certain other New Testament passages (cf. Matt. 6:2, 5, 16; Mark 14:41; Luke 6:24; Phil. 4:18; Philem. 15).

Apechō is the technical Greek word for receiving payment in full. Adolf Deissman gives many examples of this usage in both the papyri and ostraca. It is used in receipting the payment of rent, taxes, the price of a slave, or the payment of a grocery bill. In any such case the use of *apechō* means "paid in full" or "I have received all that is due me." A derivative of this verb (*apochē*) is used exactly in our sense of a "receipt."

This verb is used by Jesus three times in Matthew 6:2, 5, 16, where it is translated "They have their reward" (*apechousin ton misthon autōn*). In each instance this expression follows an example of those who practice certain righteous deeds (6:1, "alms" is "righteousness") for outward display but with no inner meaning, namely, alms, prayer, and fasting. Men give alms "that they may have glory of men" (6:2). They receive glory or praise from men, but they receive none from God. *Apechousin* . . . "Paid in full." Or they pray to be "seen of men" (6:5). Men see them. That is all. They are not seen or heard by God. *Apechousin* . . . "Paid in full." They fast "that they may appear unto men to fast" (6:16). They appear unto men to fast, but not unto God. *Apechousin* . . . "Paid in full."

So Jesus says, "They can sign the receipt of their reward." For that is all of the reward that they will receive. Their reward is from men and not from God. What a warning to search our hearts as to the motive for our deeds of righteousness! The man who depends upon outward, mechanical deeds for his salvation will do well to heed this word from Jesus (cf. Matt. 5:20-48).

A similar thought is expressed in Luke 6:24. In contrast to the blessedness of those who receive a reward in heaven for heavenly virtues and for faithfulness under persecution, Jesus says of the "rich" in things of earth, "But woe unto you that are rich! for ye have received [*apechete*] your consolation." They were "paid in full" in earth's riches, but they have no reward or consolation in heaven.

Another interesting use of this word is found in Philippians 4:18. In prison Paul had received a gift from the church at Philippi. Thus he says, "But I have all [*apechō*], and abound. . . ." In a sense this apostle is signing a receipt for the gift.

Furthermore, Paul's use of this word in Philemon 15 is significant. Philemon's slave, Onesimus, had run away to Rome where Paul led him to Christ. Now he sends him back to his master with the request that Philemon receive him as a Christian brother. In effect Paul says, "For perhaps he therefore departed for a season [you lost him temporarily as a slave], that thou shouldest receive [*apecheis*] him [as a Christian brother] for ever." Thus Philemon will receive full payment as he experiences a new relationship with Onesimus.

One of the most significant uses is found in Mark 14:41 where *apechō* is translated "it is enough." Jesus had just finished His third prayer in Gethsemane. Now He tells His sleeping disciples to "sleep on now, and take your rest: it is enough, the hour is come; . . . rise up, let us go; lo, he that betrayeth me is at hand" (vv. 41-42).

Let us reconstruct the scene. In great agony (Luke 22:44) Jesus has prayed for victory as He faces the cross. Now that victory has come to Him, He says, *Apechei* "It is enough." Several suggested meanings are offered for this.

One late manuscript reads, *Apechei to telos,* "this is the end." But this is hardly likely. Frequent uses of this word are found (*ouden apechei*) meaning "nothing hinders," suggesting of the sleeping disciples, "that is a hindrance" in this decisive moment. However, this is a strained connotation. More likely is the interpretation which makes "he that betrayeth" (v. 42) the subject of the verb *apechei*. If so, Jesus is saying, "He [Judas] did receive [the promised money]." Thus he is "paid in full." There are papyri examples to support such a meaning. William Barclay suggests that Jesus may have been saying to Judas, "Is this the payment in full which you have been looking for?" Thus he sees this possibly as a reminder that Judas still has an account to be settled with Jesus and with God."[1]

However, a more likely meaning seems to be "The account is closed." This is in keeping with the popular usage of the word *apechō*. Jesus receipts the account. That toward which Jesus has been moving is at hand. Behind Him is His earthly ministry of teaching, healing, and preaching. The temptations to avoid the cross are over. The victory has been won. So Jesus receipts this account to open another, that of the cross and the resurrection. He is about to perform that work whereby He will become our righteousness, a righteousness which through our faith in Him God will put down to our account as the righteousness of God (cf. Rom. 4:1-5).

And that will be reward enough! For we shall be "paid in full."

---

[1] *A New Testament Wordbook,* Harper New York, p. 20.

APISTEŌ

(I Am without Faith)

The verb is formed out of *pisteuō*, to believe, and the *alpha privative*, which when placed before a word gives it the opposite meaning. So *apisteō* means to disbelieve or to refuse to believe. It might well be rendered "believe not," as it is consistently translated in the New Testament (Luke 24:11, 41; Acts 28:24; Rom. 3:3; II Tim. 2:13). The corresponding idea is found in its derivatives: *apistia*, unbelief or no faith, and *apistos*, faithless. Unfortunately the English word "unbelief" is misleading, for it suggests the idea of *un*-believing something that has once been believed. In no case is this the meaning in any of these words.

Unfortunately these words are either scarce in or absent from the papyri. But enough evidence is available to illustrate the commonly held sense of their usage. *Apisteō* is found in one instance in the reading, "I will add a fact, my lord, which will, I expect excite your wonder and disbelief until we read the documents." Another simply says, "Probably you will not believe. . . ." An inscription speaks of one: "he does not believe in the healing. . . ."

Apistia is found in one illiterate papyri example (untranslated) which is regarded as a blunder in the use of Ionic Greek. But it does show the use of the word. No papyri examples are cited of *apistos*. But one inscription uses it of one who did not believe in certain cures. However, all of these examples serve to show that they refer to *no faith* rather than to a *loss of faith*.

This connotation may be consistently followed in the New Testament. *Apisteō* is used in Luke 24:11. The women's account of the resurrection seemed as the tales of hysterical women, so the apostles "did not believe" them. In Luke 24:41, "for joy" they "did not believe" even when they saw Jesus alive. It was too good to be true! In Rome some of the Jews believed the gospel and some "did not believe" (Acts 28:24). Man's failure to believe does not render faith inoperative (Rom. 3:3). This verse shows clearly the meaning of the word. Literally, "If some did not believe [*apisteō*], the no faith [*apistia*] of them does not render ineffective [*katargeō*, to make ineffective or powerless] the faith [*pistin*] of God." A similar combination is seen in II Timothy 2:13: "If we do not believe [*apisteō*, have no faith], that one [God] keeps on abiding faithful: it is impossible to deny himself." The point to note in all of these uses is that *apisteō* does not mean to lose faith but never to have it. And this is important as we note the usages of *apistos* and *apistia*.

Jesus speaks of a generation which has no faith (*apistos*, Matt. 17:17; Mark 9:19; Luke 9:41; cf. Luke 12:46). He exhorts Thomas to examine the evidence of His bodily resurrection, "and stop being without faith. . . ." (John, who places such a great emphasis upon "faith," never uses any of these words [*apisteō, apistia, apistos*] except here and in Revelation 21:8 [*apistos*].) The same thought is implied in Acts 26:8 where Paul asks Agrippa if the resurrection should be an "incredible" (*apistos*) thought. In I Corinthians *apistos* is used eleven times, and always refers to pagan people (6:6; 7:12-15; 10:27; 14:22-24; cf. II Cor. 4:4; 16:14-15; I Tim. 5:8; Titus 1:15; Rev. 21:8).

The use of *apistia* is most revealing. Jesus could do few mighty works in Nazareth because the people had "no faith" in Him (Matt. 13:58; cf. Matt. 17:20; Mark 6:6). In Mark 9:24 a father cried, "Lord, I believe; help thou my no faith." Abraham did not stagger at God's promise through "no faith," but was "strong in faith" (*pistis*) (Rom. 4:20). Israel was broken off because of "no faith" (Rom. 11:20), but will still be grafted in if they do not abide in "no faith" (Rom. 11:23). Despite the fact that Paul persecuted the church, he received mercy because he did it in a state of "no faith" in Jesus Christ.

But the most meaningful use of *apistia* is seen in Hebrews 3:12 (cf. v. 19). For on one's interpretation of 3:12 turns the entire message of Hebrews. One of the key words in this epistle is *pistis,* faith. And *apistia* is the opposite of *pistis.*

In Hebrews 3:12 the KJV reads, "Take heed, brethren, lest there be in any of you an evil heart of unbelief, in departing from the living God." The word "brethren" indicates that he is writing to Christian people, a redeemed people. He warns them against an "evil heart of unbelief." "Evil" is an adjective (*ponēra*) which in the physical sense basically means "in poor condition" or "sick." In the classics it is used of "sick eyes" or eyes in poor condition (*ponēria ophthalmōn*). So the meaning in Hebrews 3:12 may well mean a "sick heart" which is caused by "unbelief."

We have seen that *apistia* does not mean to *un*-believe something which was once believed. It means to have "no faith." And we may well translate it thusly here. But to what does "no faith" refer?

Obviously the context involves the refusal of Israel to enter the land of Canaan under God's leadership (cf. Num. 14). In Numbers 14:11 Jehovah asks, ". . . how long will it be ere they believe me. . .?", a faith which they did not yet have. So even there the problem was "no faith."

It is in this sense that we may understand "departing from" in Hebrews 3:12. This is an aorist infinitive (*apostēnai*) of *aphistēmi,* to stand off from or to revolt. From this word comes our word "apostasy" (*apostasia*). In modern terminology it means to abandon what one has professed or believed. Hence the usual interpretation of Hebrews 3:12 is that the author warns against abandoning one's Christian faith and thus being lost again. But *apostasia* is used in the papyri for "rebel." And in the context of Hebrews 3:12 it would seem likely that that thought is present in *apostēnai.*

Against this background how may we understand *apistia?* The Israelites were a redeemed people, redeemed from the slavery of Egypt. This was not a matter of *faith* but of *fact.*

So they did not *un*-believe their redemption. On the other hand, Jehovah sought to lead them *on* into Canaan, the land in which they were to achieve their purpose as a priest-nation in God's world-redemptive mission. But they rebelled or stood-off-from God as He sought to lead them in the conquest of Canaan. In short, they had *"apistia"* (no faith) in His ability to do so against the difficulties before them. They had a "sick heart of no-faith." So they rebelled against God. They did not return to Egyptian slavery (lose their redemption). But that generation spent a wasted life in wilderness wandering. It was not until the next generation that Jehovah could proceed with His purpose for these people.

Now when we apply this to Hebrews 3:12 what is the result? The author was probably an Alexandrian, and versed in the allegorical method of interpretation. It would appear, therefore, that he applies this method to the *Exodus epic*. He warns these Hebrew Christians not to let happen to them what happened to Israel. He is writing to those who have been redeemed from their sins ("brethren"). So their redemption now was not a matter of *faith* but of *fact*. The danger which they faced was not that of *un*-believing into a state of non-redemption. It was the danger of having a "sick heart of no faith" whereby they would rebel against Christ as He tried to lead them on in their Christian development and in filling their places in God's redemptive plan for all nations. *Apistias,* then, is not a faith once possessed and lost. It is a faith which they have never yet possessed.

So the warning in Hebrews 3:12 has to do not with *salvation* in the sense of redemption or the new birth, which for the Christian is a finished state. Rather it deals with *salvation* in the sense of sanctification, one's dedication to and development in God's will for every Christian; and *glorification,* or the sum-total of rewards in heaven.

Indeed, this is the message of the entire epistle to the Hebrews. On the basis of the great redemption provided in Christ, the author exhorts his readers to be faithful in fulfilling their place in God's purpose to present the gospel of redemption to all men.

So Hebrews 3:12 does not say, "Do not go back"; but, "Let us go on unto maturity" (Heb. 6:1; cf. 5:12-14). "Maturity" (perfection) is *teleios,* the goal which involves their fulfilling of God's purpose for them. A. T. Robertson points out that "go on" (*pherōmetha*) was used in the Pythagorean Schools in the sense of being borne on to a higher stage of instruction.

This agrees with the suggested meaning of Hebrews 3:12. Hebrews 3:12 warns against failing to achieve the state in which they are to fulfill God's purpose. Hebrews 6:3 speaks of the means whereby they shall arrive in that state. And the author concludes that, like Israel, if they fail it will be because of *apistia* (3:19).

APOSTASIA

(Rebellion!)

This is a substantive (noun) derived from the verb *aphistēmi.* It is a compound verb composed of *apo,* from or away from, and *histēmi,* to set, place, or stand. Literally it means to stand away or off from. In the New Testament it is variously translated as "depart" (Luke 2:37; Acts 19:9; II Cor. 12:8; II Tim. 2:19), "draw away" (Acts 5:37), "fall away" (Luke 8:13), "refrain" (Acts 5:38), "withdraw self" (I Tim. 6:5), and "depart from" (I Tim. 4:1). In the papyri it is used in sale contracts in the sense of *repelling* claimants or trespassers. A noun form *apostasion* is found in the papyri in the sense of renouncing a contract. In the New Testament it is used for a divorcement from the marriage contract (Matt. 5:31; 19:7; Mark 10:4). The basic meaning of the verb form as given in Arndt and Gingrich (*A Greek-English Lexicon*) is to cause to revolt or to mislead (cf. Acts 5:37).

This meaning is found in the papyri for *apostasia.* In one

instance it is used of the burning of certain title deeds by Egyptian "rebels" (*apostatōn*). In another rebels (*apostaseōs*) are mentioned as forcing their way into a temple. And supporting this use in the papyri is that of Plutarch who uses it in the sense of political revolt. Furthermore, this meaning is supported by Arndt and Gingrich who define *apostasia* as "rebellion, abandonment in religious sense, apostasy," citing, among other passages, Joshua 22:22, "if it be in rebellion."

The word *apostasia* occurs only twice in the New Testament (Acts 21:21; II Thess. 2:3). And the above-mentioned examples from the papyri, followed by Arndt and Gingrich, throw light upon these New Testament uses.

In Acts 21:21 Paul is accused of teaching the Jews of the dispersion to "forsake Moses, saying that they ought not to circumcise their children, neither to walk after the customs." Literally, "rebellion [*apostasian*] you teach from Moses." In other words Paul is accused of teaching rebellion against the law of Moses, and thus threatening the Jews' way of life. In this light we can well understand the violent reaction of the Jews of Jerusalem against Paul (Acts 21:27ff.).

This idea of revolt is further seen in II Thessalonians 2:3, as noted in Arndt and Gingrich. Here Paul warns these Christians not to be misled as to the second coming of Christ. That day shall not come "except there came a falling away [*hē apostasia*] first, and that man of sin [lawlessness] be revealed, the son of perdition." Later in verse 8 he describes him as "that WICKED." But the Greek words are "the lawless one" (*ho anomos*). Such terms suggest one who is in rebellion. And this coincides with the use of *apostasia* in the papyri and elsewhere. The context of II Thessalonians 2 deals with some special person in the power of Satan who leads in a religious rebellion against God (A. T. Robertson). And the use of the definite article with *apostasia* suggests some particular rebellion, not just a gradual falling away. So II Thessalonians 2:3 reads literally, "Let no one deceive you by any means: because except the rebellion come first, and the man of lawlessness be revealed. . . ."

This idea of revolt is clearly seen in the use of the verb

form as found in Acts 5:37. Speaking in defense of the apostles, Gamaliel refers to certain ones who have led rebellions
against the constituted authorities. One of these was "Judas
of Galilee [who] . . . drew away [apestēsen] much people after
him. . . ." We have noted that Arndt and Gingrich cite this
verse as an example of the meaning of rebellion. The Septuagint version uses this verb to translate Ezekiel 20:8, "But
they rebelled against me. . . ."

All of the above citations serve to throw light upon one of
the most strategic verses in the New Testament. "Take heed
[beware], brethren, lest there be in any one of you an evil
heart of unbelief, in departing from the living God" (Heb.
3:12). This is one of the proof-texts of those who hold to the
belief in apostasy in the sense of a Christian losing his salvation.

Let it be noted that "apostasy" is a derived theological
meaning of the word *apostasia*. It is not a translation of the
meaning found in the Greek word, but a transliteration of
that word which carries another meaning entirely. We have
seen that the basic meaning in both the Greek verb and noun
forms is revolt or rebellion. In that light let us examine
Hebrews 3:12.

The traditional interpretation placed upon the Epistle to
the Hebrews is that it is a warning to first-century Hebrew
Christians not to lose their salvation by apostatizing into
Judaism. But a careful reading of this epistle in its original
language suggests another meaning (see the author's *Studies
in Hebrews,* Convention Press, Nashville, 1954): a warning
against failing to fulfill their place in God's redemptive mission for a lost world.

The author was probably of the Alexandrian school which
followed the allegorical interpretation of Scripture. Thus in
Hebrews he is giving an allegorical interpretation of the
Exodus epic of the Israelites, and applies it to these Hebrew
Christians. Note that he quotes not from the Hebrew Scriptures but from the Septuagint, an Alexandrian translation
of these Scriptures into Greek.

Now looking at Hebrews 3:12 what do we find? The con-

text reflects the background of Israel's rebellion against God
at Kadesh-barnea (Num. 13-14) where Israel refused to enter
the land of Canaan, the land of her spiritual destiny. Numbers 14:9 says, "Only rebel not ye against the Lord. . . ." The
consequence of this rebellion was that a generation wandered
and died in the wilderness without achieving God's destiny
for them as a priest-nation to the rest of the world (cf. Exod.
19:1-8; Num. 14:28ff.). They did not lose their redemption out
of Egyptian bondage, but they did lose their privilege to be a
part of God's redemption purpose for other nations.

Applying these thoughts to Hebrews 3:12 the meaning of
the verse emerges. In this verse two words stand out: "unbelief" (*apistias*) and "departing from" (*apostēnai*). To comprehend these words we must render them, apart from their
English connotations, in their original form and in their own
thought context.

Apistias is the word *pistias* (faith) with the *alpha privative*
placed before the word giving it its opposite meaning. Thus
it does not mean *dis-belief* but *no faith*. Its obvious reference
is to Jehovah's question, "How long . . . ere they believe me?"
(Num. 14:11). The Israelites did not *un-believe* God's power
to redeem them from Egypt. That was now a fact which required no faith to be accepted. They had *no faith* that God
could lead them in conquering Canaan. Thus they were
hindered from achieving their spiritual destiny. The point
here is not a past faith disavowed, but a future faith not yet
expressed.

So in Hebrews 3:12 *apistias* refers not to *un-believing* in
Christ as their Saviour. Rather it means *no-faith* in Him to
lead them on to their spiritual destiny as a part of God's
redemptive purpose for others.

Apostēnai is a second aorist infinitive of the verb *aphistēmi*,
to stand off from, or to step aside from. We have seen that
its basic meaning is to cause to revolt. Keep in mind the relation of this verse to the passage in Numbers. When God
sought to lead Israel into Canaan, the Israelites stood off from
Him. They revolted or rebelled against His will and purpose
for them (cf. Num. 14:9), with the direful consequences which

followed—not a return to the bondage of Egypt, but a wasted life in the wilderness.

So the author of Hebrews draws a parallel. He warns his readers against having *no-faith* in that they *stand off from* or *rebel* against God in refusing to follow Christ in developing into the kind of a people who can be used of God in His redemptive mission for all men. The danger to them is not to return to a state of no redemption, but to that of wasted Christian lives.

Thus this verse involves not the loss of their own souls, but that of countless other souls to whom they are charged to witness. This adds infinitely to the warning found in Hebrews 3:12.

ARCHĒGOS

(Source of Our Blessings)

The word *archēgos,* is formed from *archē* (beginning, cf. John 1:1) and *agō,* to lead. It originally was an adjective in classic Greek (cf. Plato) meaning "furnishing the first cause or occasion." Thence it became a noun meaning the originator, leader, or pioneer.

In the papyri *archēgos* is found in the shouts of the populace in honor of the *pyrtanis* (a ruler) who is called *archēge tōn agathōn,* "source of our blessings." In another example it is rendered "the first shedder." Here we see both the noun and adjective forms respectively. But the word appears on the Rosetta stone (not papyri) as an official title such as "prince." On one inscription it appears as "leader." So the papyri and inscriptions agree on the meaning as of something which is first in a series of events or persons. It further appears in the sense of one who occupies a primary position of leadership or power.

There are four instances of this word in the New Testament.

And in each instance it is applied to Jesus Christ (Acts 3:15; 5:31; Heb. 2:10; 12:2).

In Acts 3:15 it is rendered "Prince," the "Prince of life." The Jews "killed the Prince of life, whom God hath raised from the dead. . . ." Bengel calls this "the magnificent antithesis." The Jews chose a murderer to be set free (Acts 3:14), and slew Him (Christ) who is the *Source* of all life and all things (cf. John 1:3-4; cf. Col. 1:14-20; Heb. 1:2f.). This agrees with the papyri usage as "source of our blessings."

In Acts 5:31 the thought is clearly that of a ruler. So "Prince" is a fitting translation here, as seen on the Rosetta stone.

But in Hebrews 2:10 the word may more likely read "Source." "Captain" carries the military or princely connotation. It makes sense here. But it is again in agreement with the papyri example of "source of our blessings." God ("him," v. 10) is seen as the *first Cause* ("for whom") and direct Agent ("by whom") of the universe (*"ta panta"*). But in Hebrews 1:2 the author has already said that Christ is the immediate Agent "through [*dia*] whom also he [God] made the ages." So in Colossians 1:16 it is said of Christ that "by him" (*en,* in the sphere of), "by him" (*dia,* through, immediate agency), and "for him" (*eis,* unto) the universe came into being. Thus Christ is the Sphere, direct Agent, and Goal of the universe. Thus we may understand *archēgos* in Hebrews 2:10 to mean that Christ is the Source of salvation, with the added meaning that He is also its immediate Agent and Goal. Arndt and Gingrich give one meaning of this word to be that of *"one who begins* something as first in a series and thus supplies the impetus." So Christ is the *archēgos* of salvation who also keeps it in effect or carries it through to completion.

In Hebrews 12:2 this same idea is present. Jesus is called "the author and finisher of *our* faith." We might well render this "the beginner and finisher of faith."

The word "author" (*archēgos*) implies source or the one who originates faith. Moffatt translates it "The pioneer of personal faith." "Finisher" is *teleiōtēn*. This is apparently a word coined by the writer from *teleioō*. (See this word later in this volume.) The Vulgate translates it "consummator." The Greek word entails the idea of the goal involving the means (*telos*) by which it is reached (cf. kindred word in 2:1). So Jesus is the source out of which faith flows. He is also the means whereby faith achieves its goal, both in the cross and resurrection and in His continuing priestly ministry "at the right hand of the throne of God." This last phrase suggests also the princely idea in *archēgos*.

So *archēgos* speaks of Christ as the Source of all life, including salvation life, and who by His priestly and ruling power carries it forward to its full and intended end. Thus in truth He is the *archēgos* or "source of our blessings."

ARRABŌN

(Earnest Money)

This word is of Semitic origin. It is a Greek transliteration of a Hebrew word meaning "pledge" (Gen. 38:17, 18, 20). In the Authorized Version of the New Testament it is rendered by the word "earnest" (II Cor. 1:22; 5:5; Eph. 1:14). However, in the more modern versions it is translated "pledge" and "installment" (Moffatt), "first installment" (Williams), and "guarantee" (RSV). These latter meanings are derived from the papyri.

In the papyri the word appears often in the sense of "earnest-money," or a down-payment which guarantees the full payment for the thing purchased. A woman selling a cow received 1000 drachmae as *arabōna* (note one "r," the exact spelling of the Hebrew word). A man gave 160 drachmae as earnest-money (*arabōnos*) in the purchase of land. One instance reads, "Regarding Lampon the mouse-catcher I paid him for you as earnest money (*arabōna*) 8 drachmae in order that he may catch the mice while they are with young." A bargain seeker! Another usage regards dancing girls engaged for a village festival. To seal the bargain they received certain drachmae "by way of earnest-money [*arabōnos*] to be reckoned in the price." One example uses *arabōna* for "the engagement ring." So in each instance the *arabōn* was "earnest-money" or a *pledge* to guarantee the fulfillment of a contract.

When this thought is applied to the New Testament usage of the word the same thought is found. Each of these is found in the writings of Paul, a Hebrew who was familiar with the current terminology of Greek life. He borrowed freely from this vocabulary to express Christian truth (cf. sports). Here he appropriates a commercial term to teach a great truth about the Holy Spirit, for each instance involves the third person of the Trinity.

In II Corinthians 1:22 he speaks of God "who hath also sealed us [another term from commercial and legal life, cf. the custom of the seal ring of the ruler], and given the earnest [*arabōna*] of the Spirit in our hearts." Again in II Corinthians 5:5, ". . . God, who also hath given unto us the earnest [*arabōna*] of the Spirit." This thought is even more clearly seen in Ephesians 1:13-14. ". . . in whom [Christ] also after that ye believed, ye were sealed with that Holy Spirit of promise, which is the earnest [*arabōn*] of our inheritance until the redemption of the purchased possession. . . ."

When Jesus died on the cross He purchased a possession for Himself. All who believe on Him become His "purchased possession." To insure His full salvation He gives the Holy Spirit in the believer's heart as "earnest-money" that He will live by His agreement to save all who believe in Him. Thus this "earnest money" involves complete salvation—regeneration, sanctification, and glorification. Redemption of the soul, salvation of the Christian life, and ultimate, complete salvation as the believer is glorified with Him (cf. Heb. 9:28; I John 5:5-12).

In the light of the one use in the papyri may it not be said that the Holy Spirit is "the engagement ring" which the Bridegroom gives to His bride looking toward the marriage feast of the Lamb (cf. Rev. 21:2)?

BEBAIOŌ

(A Title Guarantee)

As one studies the papyri and its kinship with the language of the New Testament it is everywhere evident that the Christian message was wrought out in the arena of life and is related to the needs of every man. This is clearly seen in the verb *bebaioō* and its derivatives (*bebaios, bebaiōsis*). These words carry both a legal and a commercial meaning, a legally guaranteed security. They are akin to *arrabōn* (see above). As *arrabōn* guarantees that a sale will be consummated, *bebaioō* guarantees that the terms of the sale will be kept. This latter word means "to make firm or to establish." Thus it has in it the idea of "strength."

In the papyri this verb is used in the sense of "to give a guarantee" with regard to a sale. One example reads, "If I make a claim or fail to guarantee the sale, the claim shall be invalid." Another: "will guarantee the sale with every guarantee."

The same idea is present in the use of *bebaios* which means "firm or permanent." In a figurative sense it carries the thought of "reliable, dependable." In one papyri example where one makes application for a lease, provision is made that barring an objection "the lease may remain guaranteed to us for the period of five years without change." Another:

"that those who have obtained possession may be secured in it." A very strong use of *bebaios* is seen in "and I will further guarantee [*bebaios*] the property always against all claims with every guarantee [*bebaiōsis*]". This latter word means a "confirmation" with respect to a sale. One papyri example uses it in the sense of a guarantee that there is no debt against it by the fiscal authorities.

Deissman holds that these various words must always be read with the technical sense of a guarantee in mind. A clear example of this use of *bebaioō* is seen in Romans 15:8. ". . . Jesus Christ was a minister of [to] the circumcision for the truth of God, to confirm [*bebaioō*] the promises made unto the fathers; and that the Gentiles might glorify God for his mercy. . . ." The ministry of Jesus guaranteed God's promise of redemption to both Jews and Gentiles.

The Corinthian Christians themselves are evidence of Christ's guarantee that He would save all who believe in Him (I Cor. 1:6). And He has also guaranteed that they will be unblameable or not arraigned [*anegklētous*] at the Judgment (I Cor. 1:8). The one who gives this *guarantee* (establisheth) "in [into] Christ" is God, "who hath also sealed us [for delivery], and given the earnest [*arrabōn*] of the Spirit in our hearts" (II Cor. 1:21). Note the combination of "guarantee," "seal," and "earnest money." Paul could hardly have made it any stronger. Colossians 2:7 reads "guaranteed" in the faith. And this guarantee is "in him [Christ]."

In Hebrews 2:2-3 we have both *bebaios* and *bebaioō*, "The word spoken by angels was stedfast [*bebaios*, guaranteed]." And the gospel which was first spoken by the Lord, its accuracy was guaranteed (confirmed, *bebaioō*) to the author by those who heard Him. Furthermore, these Hebrew Christians are not to be "carried about with divers and strange doctrines." Their hearts are to be established (guaranteed) by grace, not by works or by faith in Old Testament sacrifices but by the sacrifice of Christ (Heb. 13:9ff.).

Likewise do we find the use of the word *bebaios*. In Romans 4:16 the promise of redemption is guaranteed (might be sure) to the true seed of Abraham, not by works but by grace through faith. In II Corinthians 1:7 Paul knows that his hope is guaranteed (stedfast) that as the Corinthians partake of his sufferings they shall also share in his comfort or encouragement.

A very striking example of this word is seen in Hebrews 3:14: "For we are made partakers of Christ, if we hold the beginning of our confidence stedfast unto the end." "Partakers" means "partners" (cf. *metochos*). "Are made" renders one word, the perfect tense of "become," a finished work with no possibility of change. "Confidence" (*hupostaseōs*, cf. Heb. 11:1, "substance") is used in the papyri for a "title-deed." The Greek text reads, "the title-deed until the end guaranteed" (*bebaios*). "Hold" (*katechō*) means to hold down in the sense that one really has it. So the proof that one is a "partner of Christ" is that he holds a *title-deed* which is *guaranteed until the end* or with no possibility of being altered. So the thought is not that one is a partner of Christ if he holds onto his title-deed until the end of life. Rather it means that proof of this partnership lies in the fact that he really possesses this "title-deed guaranteed until the end." It is a guarantee that the title-deed stands with no possibility of being changed. The question is not will you hold on to the guaranteed title-deed, but do you really have it?

The same thought is present in Hebrews 3:6. We are the "house" of Christ if we really have (*katechō*) "the assurance [confidence] and the rejoicing of the guaranteed until the end hope" (*tēs elpidos mechri telous bebaian*). Again the thought is not that of holding on to our "assurance" and "hope" until the end of life. Rather it is the proof of our relationship to Christ in that we have this *guaranteed until the end* assurance and hope with no possibility of its being changed.

Furthermore, in Hebrews 9:17 "of force" should read "guaranteed" (*bebaios*). A will may be changed by the testator while he lives. But after his death the terms of the will are in force or *guaranteed* with no possibility of change. The death of Christ gives to us this *guarantee*.

Two final examples of *bebaios* are found in II Peter. In 1:10 Peter exhorts his readers "to make guaranteed" their calling and election. This could mean to be certain that you have this *guaranteed* promise of redemption. On the other hand in this context of *good works,* which are not a part of a salvation by grace, it probably refers to "calling and election" in the sense of their *call* and *election* as Christians to service for Christ and others. This is one very definite meaning of these words in the Bible. So the *guarantee* here is not with respect to redemption but to the saving of their Christian lives for the purpose toward which they were called or elected. The use of this word in II Peter 1:19 ("more sure," *bebaioteron*) means that the message of Peter, based upon personal experience (vv. 16-18), is *more guaranteed* of God than "cunningly devised fables" (v. 16).

Two examples of *bebaiōsis* are found in the New Testament. In Philippians 1:7 he simply states that the Philippian Christians, through their gift to Paul (1:5), share in his bonds and in his "defense [*apologiai,* apology in the forensic sense] and confirmation [*bebaiōsis,* assertion of a guarantee] of the gospel," or that the gospel is true and will perform that which Paul claims for it.

In Hebrews 6:16 is found a most interesting use of this word. Men wrangle over a sale. But when one gives a guarantee by an oath concerning his performance in it, that ends the dispute (*antilogias*). He then points out God's oath (v. 17) whereby we have "an anchor of the soul, both sure and stedfast (*bebaios,* guaranteed) (v. 19).

That which God promises He will also perform.

BAPTIZŌ

(Submerged)

Baptizō and its kindred words (*baptisma, baptismos, baptistēs*) are found often in the Christian's vocabulary. *Baptizō* basically means to dip or immerse. *Baptistēs* is simply a surname as of John the Baptist (cf. Matt. 3:1; Mark 6:14 the word is "the one baptizing). The nouns *baptisma* and *baptismos* are rendered "baptism," but basically mean a dipping or immersion.

Baptizō occurs eighty times in the New Testament. Quite obviously it is not found so often in the papyri. But there are examples of its various usages as found in the New Testament. As late as the fourth century A.D. it is used of a "submerged" boat, which confirms its basic meaning. Josephus (not papyri) uses it in the first century A.D. for what we would call "ducking" a man until he was drowned.

Moulton and Milligan list two papyri examples where the reference is to ceremonial ablutions. A further example is cited in a very illiterate letter where one speaks of being "flooded" or overwhelmed with calamities (cf. Mark 10:38).

Only one example of *baptisma* is listed by Moulton and Milligan. But it is significant. "What is the new baptism that they say thou dost preach?" Here it is clear that *baptisma* refers to the meaning and not to the act of baptism. Understandably this word is found only in New Testament and ecclesiastical writings.

Not so with *baptismos*. There is no known example of this word in ecclesiastical writings with reference to Christian baptism unless we so read Hebrews 6:2. Nor does it appear in the papyri. But in Josephus it is used with reference to

John's baptism. At one time it was thought to be the only use of this word by a profane writer. But one example has been found in the writings of Plutarch, where it (*baptismous*) is called a *superstition*. It appears in the New Testament in reference to the *act* of baptism or of Jewish ceremonial washings or ablutions (Mark 7:4; Heb. 6:2; 9:10). It is generally agreed that *baptisma* refers to the meaning of baptism, and *baptismos* connotes the act itself.

We shall not endeavor to treat every example of *baptizō* in the New Testament. In most instances the context makes clear the meaning. But several usages call for consideration.

For instance, its use for "wash" in Mark 7:4 and Luke 11:38 refers to Jewish ceremonialism. The thought is that of dipping or submerging the hands or vessels in water. Note "washings" in Mark 7:4 (*baptismos*). The thought back of this was not physical cleanliness. Instead, it was that demons got on the hands or vessels and thence through the mouth into the body.

The thought of being "flooded" or overwhelmed with calamity is reflected in Jesus' words to James and John (Mark 10:38-39; cf. Luke 12:50; note Matt. 20:20-23 not in best mss.). In both Mark and Luke "baptism" is *baptisma,* referring to the meaning of the act.

Perhaps the clearest New Testament passage with respect to the meaning of baptism is seen in Romans 6:3-5. Here both the verb (*baptizō*) and the noun (*baptisma*) are used. Thus baptism (*baptisma*) is pictured as a burial and a resurrection. Therefore, baptism is shown to be a picture or symbol of that which Christ did for our salvation, death, burial, and resurrection. It also depicts that which happens to the believer: death and burial of the old life, and the resurrection to walk in a new life in Christ (cf. Col. 2:12). It also portrays the believer's faith in the final resurrection from the dead (v. 5).

Perhaps a good literal translation of Romans 6:3-5 might read: "Do you not know that so many as are baptized with respect to [*eis*] Christ ["Jesus" not in best mss.], with respect to his death are baptized? Therefore we are buried with him through the meaning of baptism with respect to death: in order that as Christ was raised up out of the realm of the dead through the glory of the Father, even so we also in the sphere of [*en*] newness of life should walk. For if we have been planted together in the likeness of his death, we shall be also *in the likeness* of the [his] resurrection."

In this connection it is well to examine Acts 2:38, "baptized . . . for the remission of sins. . . ." "For" is *eis* which may be variously rendered "into, unto, for, with respect to, at, on the basis of, as a result of." This same word in Luke 11:32 is rendered "they repented at [*eis*] the preaching of Jonah." Here the idea clearly is that of result. They repented not in order that Jonah might preach, but because or after he had preached. The English word "for" is also used in this sense. "He was executed *for* murder." Not in order that he might murder, but because he had murdered. In the light of the teaching of the New Testament with respect to salvation by grace, this is a consistent meaning in Acts 2:38. ". . . be baptized . . . as the result of the remission of sins. . . ."

One of the most difficult passages in the New Testament is I Corinthians 15:29, "Else what shall they do which are baptized for the dead, if the dead rise not at all? why are they then baptized for the dead?" There are more than fifty different interpretations which are offered concerning this verse. The problem hinges on the words "dead" and "for." Some hold the meaning to be "baptized with respect to dead works." But "dead" is masculine, so it must refer to persons. The word "for" (*huper*) may be translated "over," "in the place of," or "on behalf of." The ancients (Tertullian) held to the idea of being baptized in the place of people already dead so that they might be saved. Since this practice did not begin until a century after Paul wrote this, we must look elsewhere for the meaning.

Others emphasizing the word "over," hold that it referred to one being baptized over the body of the dead for his salvation. But A. T. Robertson says that there is no example of the purely local use of *huper* in the New Testament.[2] Furthermore, he points out several meanings of *huper* with the *abla-*

---

[2] *A Grammar of the Greek New Testament,* Doran, 1923, p. 632.

tive case, as here: "in behalf of," "instead," "for the sake of," "about," or "concerning." He holds to the last word here.

However, when we keep in mind the figure of baptism in Romans 6:3-5 and Colossians 2:12 Paul's meaning seems to come into focus. He is speaking of death and the resurrection as symbolized in baptism. Therefore, "dead" may well refer to the believer who has died to his old life. In baptism he symbolizes its burial and the resurrection to a new life in Christ. In effect, Paul says that if there be no resurrection, then the very symbol of baptism is meaningless. For a fuller discussion of this problem see Hobbs, *Messages on the Resurrection,* Baker, pp. 49ff.

Now briefly let us examine *baptismos* and *baptisma.* We have seen that the former word refers to the act of baptism. In the Authorized Version it is used in Mark 7:4 (not in best mss. of Mark 7:8) and Hebrews 9:10 as "washing," referring to Jewish ceremonial ablutions, not to Christian baptism. The one possible Christian usage is in Hebrews 6:2. Since it is a plural form even here it may refer to Jewish ablutions which possibly had been retained in the teachings of these Hebrew Christians. Even if it refers to the Christian ordinance, it speaks of the act not its meaning.

All other uses of "baptism" in the New Testament render *baptisma,* the meaning of baptism. In this light let us examine two uses only. In Acts 19:3-4 the word appears twice. Clearly the thought here is that of *meaning* as seen in verse 4. John's baptism was administered on the basis of repentance and a willingness to participate in the coming Kingdom of God. These disciples of John knew nothing of the ministry of Jesus, especially of His death and resurrection. They had probably been *won* by Apollos, an Alexandrian Jew, who was "mighty in the Scriptures" (Old Testament) and who knew only "the baptism of John" (cf. Acts 18:24-25). Thus he needed instruction in "the way of God more perfectly" (v. 26). These disciples, after they heard (and believed) the gospel of Christ, were baptized with Christian baptism symbolizing that which it portrayed (cf. Rom. 6:3-5).

The other use of *baptisma* to be noted is in I Peter 3:21:

"The like figure ["water" in v. 20] whereunto even baptism doth also now save us. . . ." This refers to the *meaning* not the *act* of baptism. Drawing on the figure of Noah being saved "through [*dia*] water," he is simply saying that believers are also saved by the *meaning (baptisma)* symbolized by the ordinance of baptism, the death, burial, and resurrection of Christ. That this is not a *sacrament* is evident in the words "not the putting away of the filth of the flesh" as seen in the Jewish ablutions *(baptismos)*.

CHARTĒS

(Writing Paper)

A volume of this kind would hardly be complete without this word. It is the word for "papyrus." In the papyri it is sometimes used for papyrus rolls: "I shall require 4 papyrus rolls for these things." Or it may be employed for single sheets of paper: "I bought two sheets of paper." An interesting use of a kindred word, *chartion,* reads, "Not having found a clean sheet of paper, for the moment I have written on this."

This word *(chartēs)* appears only one time in the New Testament (II John 12). Instead of writing more "with paper and ink," he plans to visit "the elect lady and her children" [a church?] and deliver his message in person.

But the point of interest is that John did write II John on a sheet of papyrus, using black ink *(melas* means "black"). The length of this letter would indicate that he used a single sheet, as also for III John.

The length of I John and his Gospel would seem to indicate that he used papyrus rolls of different lengths. John 20:30 indicates that he wrote on papyrus or a "scroll," a roll of papyrus.

Indeed, the oldest known New Testament document is a papyri fragment of a portion of John's Gospel now in the John Rylands Library, Manchester, England. Three leading papyrologists (Bell, Kenyon, Schubart) agree in dating this in the first quarter of the second century (circa A.D. 98-117). Schubart is inclined to date it in the closing years of the first century (A.D. 81-96), the very period in which this Gospel probably was written.

CHEIROGRAPHON

(A Certificate of Debt)

This very interesting word appears only one time in the New Testament (Col. 2:14). But it is found often in the papyri. Literally, it means "written with the hand" or "a signature" (cf. Gal. 6:11). But in a more technical sense it connotes "a written agreement," "a certificate of debt," or a "bond."

Examples from the papyri read: "for which you drew me up a *bond*," in connection with a purchase of wine; "let this *bond* written by me in duplicate be valid" (cf. Philem. 18f.); "the capital sum lent to you by me in accordance with a *note in hand*" (author's italics). A note of humor appears in the following, "If you can, please worry Dioscorus and exact from him his bond." More to the point of Colossians 2:14 is "being therefore desirous that the authentic bond should be publicly registered."

In Colossians 2:14 the word appears in the following phrase, "Blotting out the *handwriting* of ordinances [Mosaic law] that was against us . . ." (author's italics). "Handwriting" is a *cheirographon*, or a certificate of debt "against us." On the cross Christ *blotted it out,* nailing it to the cross as a public registration that it had been paid.

This figure of "blotting out" is well authenticated in the papyri. One example reads, "a decree [*cheirographon*] neither washed out nor written over." In the same vein are two others: "both crossed out and cancelled;" or in connection with the trial of the governor of Egypt, "gave orders that the bond be crossed out." Many papyri examples have been "crossed out" thus, "X," as we do today, so cancelled.

The word for "blotted out" means to rub out, wipe off, or erase (cf. also Acts 3:19; Rev. 3:5). Plato used this word of blotting out a writing. Sometimes manuscripts were rubbed or scraped and written over again. All of these thoughts add meaning to Paul's phrase.

When Christ was nailed to the cross our certificate of indebtedness was taken out of the way (cf. John 1:29). Literally, "out of the way" means "out of the midst." So the certificate of our indebtedness, the law and its attendant sin, that which stood in the midst or in between us and God, was washed out, written over, or crossed out so that there is "nothing between my soul and the Saviour."

CHORTAZŌ

(Satisfied but Hungry)

The basic meaning of this verb is "to feed to the full" or "to satisfy." Modern Greek uses it in the sense of "satiate." In its original sense it referred to animals, but gradually came to be applied to men in the sense of "eat." Moulton and Milligan list only one use of this verb in a papyri example dated 254 B.C. But numerous examples are found of two noun forms: *chortasma,* "food," "sustenance" (cf. Acts 7:11;

but in the Septuagint for fodder for domestic animals); *chortos,* "grass," "hay" (cf. Matt. 14:19; John 6:10).

From the above it is to be expected that in the New Testament the word would be found in both the vulgar [animal] and the refined [man] sense. In the latter sense it is used in Matthew 5:6 where Arndt and Gingrich render it "be satisfied" (cf. Luke 6:21). But even here the thought is to be fed to the full.

Various uses are found in the accounts of the feeding of the multitudes where they were fed to the full (Matt. 14:20; 15:33, 37; Mark 6:42; 8:8; Luke 9:17; 16:21; James 2:16). The abundance of the miracles is seen not only in the *leftovers* but in the satiated stomachs.

In Philippians 4:12 is found Paul's only use of the word, which Nägeli calls "one of the few vulgarism Paul permits himself." The apostle notes his good times and his bad ones. He says, "I am disciplined to be full and to be hungry." "To be full" is the word. It could well be rendered "to have a full stomach." The thought is prosperity. The Orientals say that a man is prosperous when he is full of rice. Note the Buddha's *prosperous* stomach.

But the strictly vulgar sense of this word is found in the writings of John, one of the most spiritually sensitive of all New Testament writers. Note Revelation 19:21. Arndt and Gingrich catch the animal aspect of its meaning when they translate it "all the birds gorged themselves with their flesh." This renders a passive form of the verb which, according to Arndt and Gingrich, means to eat one's fill. Hence, to gorge one's self.

It is of interest to note that John's only other use of this verb is in John 6:26. "Ye seek me, not because ye saw the miracles [signs], but because ye did eat of the loaves, and were filled." "Were filled" is also a passive form. So Jesus, in effect, said, "Ye gorged yourselves on the loaves, but paid no heed to the signs of my deity." Like animals they filled their stomachs to the full, but left their souls empty. They did not ask whence came the food, nor for what purpose it was given. They sought Jesus now only because it was breakfast time, and they were hungry again. When Jesus offered them heavenly bread instead of bread for their stomachs, they left Him.

History records that Nero sought to gain favor with the Roman populace by giving them free bread. When ships arrived from Egypt, which they thought contained wheat, but carried sand for his circus, the multitude turned on him.

Jesus refused to be merely a filler of stomachs. Instead, He came to minister to the soul. Even when He spoke of eating His flesh, these carnal people could rise in thought no higher than their stomachs (cf. John 6:52). Alas, how many people think of Jesus and the gospel only in terms of their creature comforts. For this reason Jesus says, "Ye have no life in you" (John 6:53).

DIATHĒKĒ

(Testament, Will)

This word comes from the verb *diatithēmi* which variously means to issue a decree, conclude an agreement, assign or confer, and to dispose of property by a will. So a *diathēkē* was the instrument by which any of these actions was performed. In the Old Testament (Septuagint) it is used consistently to translate the Hebrew word *berith* which means "covenant," such as the covenant with Noah, Abraham, or Moses. This usage is carried over into the New Testament, where the word is rendered thirteen times as "covenant." But the other twenty uses translate it as "testament." It is used in religious language for Old and New Testaments.

To understand this word it must be compared with another word, *sunthēkē*, which does not appear in the New Testament. A *sunthēkē* (note *sun*, with), an agreement entered into by equals. The verb form is found in Luke 22:5. Judas had something that the chief priests wanted (information); the chief priests had something that Judas wanted (money). So on equal terms they "covenanted" or entered into an agreement.

But *diathēkē* means an agreement entered into by two parties which are unequal. The superior party sets forth an agreement under terms of his own choosing, which the inferior party may either accept or reject, but cannot alter. Should the latter fail to keep the terms of the covenant, it becomes null and void.

To understand fully the use of *diathēkē* in the New Testament it is necessary to examine the covenant relationship in the Old Testament.

The translators of the Septuagint chose this word to render the Hebrew word *berith*. But the conditional element is absent from the covenant with Noah. It is more of an arbitrary "promise" or decree made by God, with no conditions attached (Gen. 9:11ff.).

In the case of the Abrahamic covenant (Gen. 12:1-3)[3] the conditional element is not readily seen, unless one regards "thou shalt be a blessing . . .and in thee shall all families of the earth be blessed" as such. The outward evidence of this covenant was the rite of circumcision (Gen. 17:10). It involved the occupation of the land of Canaan (Gen. 17:8), but this was not a condition of it. Nevertheless God called it an "everlasting covenant, to be a God unto thee, and to thy seed after thee." But this is the promise, not the condition.

The significance of this fact is seen in that the covenant with Abraham was one of redemption, the conditions of which would be fulfilled in Christ the true seed of Abraham (cf. Gal. 3:16). Men would fulfill these conditions by being "in Christ" through faith. Therefore, the significance of the absence of conditions not stated but implied is that this was a covenant of grace (cf. Rom. 4), a gift-covenant, hence an "everlasting covenant."

[3] The author is assuming that the basic element of God's covenant is found in Genesis 12:1-3. Genesis 15 and 17:7-14 are but subsequent elements of this basic promise.

The clearest Old Testament example of a conditional covenant is that which God made with Israel (Exod. 19:5-8). Note the "if" and "then" in verse 5. These were conditions to be kept by man. It was a covenant of law. And when Israel failed to keep the condition (to be a priest-nation), the covenant was disannulled. Thus God made a new covenant (cf. Jer. 31; Matt. 21:43-45; Heb. 8:6ff.) "established upon better promises" (Heb. 8:6). This latter statement harks back to the promise made to Abraham (Gen. 12:1-3) which is to be realized through his "seed" (Gen. 17:7f.), even Christ (Gal. 3:16). Thus the Abrahamic covenant of grace is basic in God's redemptive purpose.

But to comprehend the use of *diathēkē* in the New Testament it is also vital that we examine it in its setting contemporary with both the Septuagint and the New Testament. This is found in the papyri.

The Septuagint was translated in the third century B.C. in an environment where the Greek language was current. It is to be expected, therefore, that the translators would choose a word whose current meaning was similar to that which they understood to be in the Hebrew *berith*. Although the New Testament was written some three centuries later the same language was current. And the tie that binds these two bodies of Biblical literature together linguistically is found in the papyri. For this reason the papyri throws a flood of light on the meaning of *diathēkē*.

According to Moulton and Milligan in the papyri the word means "testament" or "will" with absolute unanimity. Of interest is the fact that *sunthēkē* is used of a "compact" between equals; *diathēkē* of a will between unequals. The verb form *diatithēmi* is used in the regular formula for making a will.

The oldest papyri example (236 B.C.) of *diathēkē*, which is almost contemporary with the Septuagint, reads, "I leave behind the testament" (will). Many similar examples are found in the Septuagint period. That the same thought extends into the New Testament period is seen in a 14 B.C. example of a strictly Jewish usage. It reads, "According to

which he made a will through the high priest of the Jews."
One papyri example of the use of the verb form *(diatithēmi)*
is seen in the word "intestate" *(adiathetos)*, dying without
making a will. All of these papyri uses are also found in
various ancient inscriptions.

So it is quite clear that *diathēkē* in the papyri carries the
idea of one making a will containing conditions of his own
choosing, with others as beneficiaries, who may either accept
or reject the conditions, but cannot alter them. This thought
must have been in the minds of the Septuagint translators
when they chose *diathēkē* to render *berith*.

However, in the New Testament scholars are divided as to
the meaning of *diathēkē*. Westcott, followed by Moulton,
insists that "covenant" must stand everywhere. Deissmann
seems to favor "testament" or "will." Milligan formerly held
with Westcott. But, in the light of the papyri, he later came
to the position that the context must decide in every case.

Certainly where the word translates or refers to the Hebrew word *berith*, "covenant" should be understood (cf. Luke
1:72; Acts 3:25; 7:8; Heb. 8:9). But even here the thought of
a "testament" is not entirely absent. However, as Moulton
and Milligan note it is difficult to see that the uses of Paul, a
Jew "with the Greek language in the very fibre of his
thought," and the author of Hebrews, who consistently quotes
from the Septuagint, do not reflect a consciousness of the
Greek connotation of the word as "testament" along with the
Hebrew idea of "covenant." An examination of their usage
of *diathēkē* shows that they do intermingle the two ideas.

In Galatians 3:15-17 a man makes a "will" which can be
neither disannulled nor added to by the beneficiary (Greek
idea). This Paul likens to the "promises" made to Abraham
and his (spiritual) seed (Hebrew concept). This "will" God
confirmed in Christ (v. 16). God set the conditions, and Christ
fulfilled them. All who receive Christ fulfil the conditions in
Him. This "will" cannot be set aside by the covenant made
under the law (v. 17). The covenant with Israel (Exod. 19:5-8)
was an "if" and "then" covenant made between God and man,
and which involved service, not redemption. Israel's failure

did disannul this covenant made under law. Elsewhere this
covenant of service was made with the church (Matt. 21:43-45;
I Peter 2:9-10).

But the law did not disannul the covenant or "will" with
Abraham (Heb. 2:16-18). This was a covenant of redemption,
and, therefore, of grace. Instead, Christ, the true seed of
Abraham (Gal. 3:16), fulfilled its conditions. He, thus, is the
end (fulfilment) of the law unto righteousness for those who
believe in Him (Rom. 10:4), both Jew and Gentile. Therefore,
the "promises" made to Abraham (Gen. 12:1-3) are more in
the nature of a "will" or "testament" given by grace to those
who through faith in Christ become sons of God. And this is
an everlasting covenant.

Further light is shed on this use of *diathēkē* in Ephesians
2:12-13. Paul refers to the time when the Gentiles were
"aliens from the commonwealth of Israel, and strangers from
the covenants of promise. . . ." "Commonwealth of Israel"
refers to the Mosaic covenant made with the nation Israel.
"Covenants of promise" involve both the Abrahamic and
Mosaic covenants. However, the weight of Old Testament
teaching is that the Mosaic covenant was made with a true
people of God, excluding even Israelites who did not fall into
this category. So Paul may be understood as referring to the
spiritual or true Israel or true "seed" of Abraham (cf. Rom.
9:6-8).

It was the true seed of Abraham which was included in
God's "promises" or "will." The pagan world, therefore, was
outside the family of God, not His children, and, therefore,
not included in His "will." However, through Christ the
"seed" (Gal. 3:16) they may become children of God, "heirs
of God, and joint-heirs with Christ" (Rom. 8:17) in the "will"
of the Father.

The combination of the Greek and Hebrew ideas in *diathēkē* is most abundantly found in Hebrews (cf. 8:6-10; 9:4;
10:16, 29; 12:24; 13:20). In these passages the author refers
to first one "covenant" and then another (Abraham, Moses,
Jer. 31, Christ). But the Mosaic covenant is presented in contrast with the others which the author views as progressive

phases of the basic covenant or "testament" made with Abraham. The governing thought is that the "promises" (8:6) made to Abraham and his "seed" are basic, and are fulfilled in Christ. The believer fulfils them through his faith whereby he is "in Christ."

But this combination of the Greek and Hebrew ideas is best seen in Hebrews 7:22; 9:15-20; and 11:19 where *diathēkē* is rendered "testament." In 7:22 the author speaks of Christ as "a surety of a better testament." The word "surety" renders a word (*egguos*) as an adjective meaning "under good security," or as a noun (as here) meaning a "guarantee." So the "will" of God is under good security with Christ as the guarantee that its terms will be carried out.

In Hebrews 9:15-20 the "new testament" in Christ is contrasted with the "first testament" (covenant) of the law (cf. 9:20). The conditions of the "new testament" are met in Christ, and therefore it abides. Those of the "first testament" were not met by men, and therefore it was disannulled. Hence the "new testament" (Jer. 31). The "promise of eternal inheritance" suggests the "promises" made to Abraham (Gen. 12:1-3). Thus once again the "will" of God is related to His covenant with Abraham, the conditions of which were fulfilled by Abraham's "seed," Christ.

But the Greek idea stands out in this passage where the author says that a "testament" or will is not in force until after the death of the "testator" (Heb. 9:16f.). This, of course, relates to the "new testament" being sealed in the death of Christ. Combined with the Hebrew idea of the covenant being sealed in blood (9:19f.) is the Greek thought contained in *diathēkē* as a "will" which does not become effective until after the death of the one making the will.

Note that in the basic covenant made with Abraham (Gen. 12:1-3) there is no sacrifice to seal it. Covenants were sometimes made by verbal agreement alone. In Genesis 15 a sacrifice is made, but it involves the seed of Abraham inheriting the land of Canaan. If we regard Genesis 12:1-3 as the basic element in the Abrahamic covenant, then it is significant that no sacrifice is made. This covenant or "testament" was to be sealed in the sacrifice of Christ on the cross.

Therefore, the "will" which God made through Abraham (Gen. 12:1-3), and whose conditions were fulfilled in Christ, became effective through the death of the Testator, even God, who was in Christ reconciling the world unto Himself (II Cor. 5:19-21). Thus the "testament" made with Abraham is sealed through the blood of Christ, and is, therefore, "the everlasting covenant" or testament (Heb. 13:20).

Is your name written in God's last "will and testament?"

DOKIMAZŌ

(Trial by Fire)

This verb and its derivatives primarily carry the meaning of "testing" in order to prove the quality of a person or thing. The verb appears twenty-three times in the New Testament, and is translated variously as "prove," "try," "approve," "discern," "allow," "like," and "examine." But in each instance it expresses the idea of a process or result of severe testing or examination. The severity of the test may be seen in I Corinthians 3:13, ". . . and the fire shall try [dokimasei] every man's work of what sort it is."

In the papyri this idea of "testing" is abundantly illustrated: "his excellency the epistrategus shall sift [dokimasei] the matter with the utmost equity" (cf. I Cor. 3:13); "in order that you may judge [dokimasēi] of his present condition"; "that after inquiry [dokimasas] you may write to me whether it is so." This last form is used of the inspection of calves for sacrifice as to whether or not they are clean or fit for that purpose.

From these uses it was a natural transition to the meaning

of "approve." Thus an early (311 B.C.) marriage contract provides that differences between the man and wife shall be settled by three persons "whom both shall approve" [*dokimazōsin*]. One instance employs this verb of those who have "passed the examination." Thus in one inscription it refers to a "character certificate" as of one fit for public office.

These uses throw light on its various meanings in the New Testament. For instance, in II Corinthians 8:8 Paul speaks of "the sincerity of your love" standing the *test* (prove) through their actions. And in 8:22 he says that after severe testing Titus has been found "diligent in many things." Thus Paul gives him a character certificate before the Corinthian Christians. In II Corinthians 13:5 and Galatians 6:4 Paul proposes that each person shall "sift" himself to see if he passes the examination. In I Corinthians 11:28 he urges this test, to determine one's motive in partaking of the Lord's Supper. "Unworthily" (v. 29) is an adverb of manner referring to the method and motive, not to personal character. I Timothy 3:10 proposes this severe test before a man is made a deacon. Men are to be so tested before being entrusted with the Lord's money (I Cor. 16:3).

In I Thessalonians 2:4 this word appears twice in a most revealing manner. "But as we were allowed [*dedokimasmetha,* perfect tense of completeness, tested and found true] of God to be put in trust [entrusted] with the gospel, even so we speak; not as pleasing men, but God, which trieth [*dokimazonti*] our hearts." Paul proposes to live up to the quality which God has found in him after severe testing, and who continues to test our motives and efforts.

Further light is shed on Hebrews 3:9. "When your fathers tempted [*peirazō*, another word for "testing"] me, proved [literally "in *dokimasia*," in severe testing] me, and saw my works. . . ." Despite the fact that they put God to the test in His works, and found Him worthy of approval, they rebelled against Him. Hence a sin of full knowledge; thus God's wrath upon them.

This verb is most expressive in I John 4:1. Christians are

not to be taken in by "every spirit." They are to put each to severe testing to be certain that it is of God or the Holy Spirit. The New Testament teaches that there are evil spirits as well as the Holy Spirit. Christians are to discern between them, a warning which is much needed today.

From the verb *dokimazō* come other words of great interest. For instance, *dokimē* (not found in the papyri) means "the quality of being approved." Hence in Romans 5:4 "experience" means "character," the result of patient endurance in trial which produces "hope" (cf. Phil. 2:22; II Cor. 2:9, "proof" means "character"; II Cor. 9:13, "experiment" means "the approved character of your service," Arndt and Gingrich). The idea of severe testing is expressed in II Corinthians 8:2 where "trial" may well be rendered "ordeal."

Another most significant derivative of *dokimazō* is *dokimios*. About this word centers one of the most dramatic stories to come out of textual criticism. This word appears in I Peter 1:7 where the Authorized Version renders it "trial." Before the relation of the papyri to the New Testament was discovered by Deissmann, Dr. Hort could find no parallel meaning of this word in the sense of this passage. Therefore, he suggested that the true text should read *dokimon*, that which is approved after trial. But the papyri revealed this very word, *dokimios* as used of the result of gold being tried in the fire, *chrusos dokimios*, "tested gold." One papyri example renders it as "standard gold," or that which came up to the approved standard. The noun form *dokimeion* is used for "crucible," the instrument in which the testing by fire was done.

Thus from the papyri it has been determined that I Peter 1:7 means "tested" or "standard" faith, that which has been tested in the "crucible" by fire and found to be genuine or "without alloy" (Arndt and Gingrich). Note that in this verse are found both the noun "trial" and the verb "tried" with fire. This same noun (*dokimion*) appears in James 1:3 with the same meaning.

So when God permits the Christian to pass through the fire it is to prove his faith to be genuine or without alloy. It is this conviction which enables one to enjoy "patience" or "manly endurance" by which victory is assured (cf. I John 5:4-5).

ENTUGCHANŌ

(Intercession)

The basic meaning of this verb is to meet, turn to, approach, appeal, or petition by one on behalf of another. When used in the religious sense it means to pray or to make intercession. Indeed the noun form (*enteuxis*) is rendered as "intercessions" (I Tim. 2:1) and "prayer" (I Tim. 4:5). In the papyri it appears repeatedly as a "petition" sent to a king or other ruler.

The papyri examples show the verb form used in both the legal and religious sense. In the legal usage are such examples as: "the 13 komo-grammateis *appealed* to the dioecetes"; "on learning this my client *appealed* to T."; "on behalf of whom he *appealed* to Apollonion." In the hostile sense of an accusation this verb is used followed by the preposition *kata* (cf. Rom. 11:2) as in "We intreated against you concerning the learouron" (?).

One classic religious example has a familiar New Testament sound. "Knowing that *night and day* I intercede before God on behalf of you" (cf. I Tim. 5:5, author's italics).

These foregoing usages shed light on the New Testament passages where this verb appears.

For instance, two uses of this verb are found in the hostile sense, one strictly legal and the other in reference to prayer. In Acts 25:24 the rendering is "dealt." Festus tells king Agrippa that the Jews have "dealt" with him concerning Paul, asking that he be executed. Here the sense is definitely that of a legal accusation. In Romans 11:2 Elijah is mentioned as "making intercession to God against Israel." This is the exact form found in the papyri for a hostile accusation (*entugchanō kata*; 11:2, *entugchanei toi Theōi kata tou Israēl*). In the religious sense the verb is translated "to make intercession." So here it is used for a prayer not on behalf of (*huper*) but against (*kata*) someone. This combines both the legal and religious sense as found in the papyri.

This combination is also seen of intercession in the good sense or on behalf of one. In Romans 8:27 the Holy Spirit is said to *make intercession* for the saints (*kata Theon entugchanei huper agiōn*). The word *huper* shows that this is intercession *on behalf of* the saints (cf. papyri example, "night and day I intercede [make intercession] to God on behalf of [*huper*] you"). *Kata Theon* may mean "according to the will of God" as in the King James Version. But used with *entugchanō* which involves coming before one on behalf of another, it more likely means "before God." This is a legitimate use of the word *kata* followed by the accusative case, as here, and it coincides with the usage in the papyri. So this verse involves one coming before God or God's throne (legal sense) in prayer (religious sense).

In this dual sense the verb is also used of Christ in Romans 8:34, ". . . who is also at the right hand of God, who also *maketh intercession* for us" (author's italics). The place is *beside* the throne, but the sense of place is evident. However, this same verb is used in Hebrews 7:25 in the strictly religious sense. Here Christ our High Priest is seen as before the altar or in the heavenly Holy of Holies *making intercession on our behalf*.

A point of interest is the word for "maketh intercession" in Romans 8:26. It is our verb prefixed by the word *huper* which in this sense means *above* or *beyond* (*huperentugchanō*). When we cannot find words to express the prayer that is in our hearts, the Holy Spirit before the throne of God *makes intercession* in our place with unutterable groanings or words *above* and *beyond* our ability to pray.

While the word *entugchanō* does not appear elsewhere in

the New Testament, the idea is present in the intercessory work of both Christ and the Holy Spirit. In the strictly legal sense it is suggested in Jesus' promise that when the apostles are brought into court the Holy Spirit will appear on their behalf, giving them the words which they shall speak (Mark 13:11).

A combination of the legal and religious usages is found in the word *paraclete (paraklētos)*. This word means a lawyer, especially for the defense, who is called to stand alongside one when he appears before the tribunal of the court. In John (14:16, 26; 15:26; 16:7) it is used of the Holy Spirit, and is rendered "Comforter." In I John 2:1 it speaks of Christ as our "advocate" before the Father. Thus the Holy Spirit is God's "advocate" or "counsellor" before the tribunal of men's hearts. Christ is our "advocate" or counsellor before the throne of God. The context of the various uses of this word in the New Testament is highly suggestive of the corresponding examples of *entugchanō* found in the papyri.

EPITHUMIA

(Running with the Wrong Crowd)

This is basically a good word which has fallen into bad company. It comes from *epithumeō* which basically means "I desire." Eight times it is so translated (Matt. 13:17; Luke 16:21; 17:22; 22:15; I Tim. 3:1; Heb. 6:11; I Peter 1:12; Rev. 9:6). Three times it is rendered "covet" (Acts 20:33; Rom. 7:7; 13:9), and three times it reads "lust" (I Cor. 10:6; Gal. 5:17; James 4:2). Once it reads "lust after" (Matt. 5:28). And one use renders it "fain" (Luke 15:16) with reference to hunger. But the idea in the word itself is "desire" in the sense of the physical appetite. Within themselves they are

God-given desires. Where the word is rendered "covet," "lust," or "lust after" it speaks of natural desires which have been perverted to evil purposes.

There are several examples of this word in the papyri. Most of the usages occur in incomplete sentences difficult to reproduce. But one example dated A.D. 2/3 reads, "I greet you, mother, through this letter, desiring now to see you." This illustrates the basic idea of desire in a good sense.

But whereas the verb form is used in the New Testament largely in the good sense, the noun form, *epithumia,* is found largely in the evil sense of "lust." Out of thirty-eight times that it appears, thirty-five of these are rendered "lust," "concupiscence" or "lust after." Three times it is translated "desire" in the good sense. However, there are two uses as "lust" which may well be rendered "desire" in the neutral sense. For instance, this seems to fit Mark 4:19. The question is whether or not one *desires* or *lusts after* "other things." (See later for James 1:14-15.)

Moulton and Milligan list no use of this word in the evil sense. It is simply "desire" in the good sense of the word. For instance, one example reads, "And then we shall be able to buy cheaply in accordance with your desire." Another: a forsaken husband is described as "loving, frantic, sleepless with love and desire for her." The negative form of the verb (*athumeō*) is found with the meaning of "draw back" or "hesitate" as one who had no desire.

Now the question is as to the difference in meaning of these two words in the New Testament. Nine out of sixteen times that *epithumeō* is used it carries the idea of wholesome "desire." But at least thirty-three out of thirty-eight times *epithumia* is found in the evil sense of "lust." This difference is especially interesting since the papyri examples cited always use both words in the good sense. May we not say that with three, and possibly five exceptions, in the New Testament the word *epithumia* has fallen into bad company?

For instance in Philippians 1:23 Paul speaks of "having a desire to depart, and to be with Christ; which is far better." And in I Thessalonians 2:17 he "endeavoured the more abundantly to see your face with great desire." A striking example of this word in the good sense is seen in Luke 12:15. Jesus says. "With *desire* I have *desired* to eat this passover with you before I suffer" (author's italics). This might well read, "I have heartily desired. . . ." Note both the noun and the verb.

And yet with possibly two exceptions this word is used elsewhere to render the word "lust" in the sense of evil desire. A study of this fact gives us a good understanding of the nature of temptation.

Too often we think of Satan as tempting us in our baser nature. And thus he disarms us at the very beginning. We look at the finished product of evil rather than at the raw materials out of which it comes. For instance, the word "tempt" really means "to try or test in order to prove." God "tempted" or tested Abraham to prove him faithful (cf. Gen. 22:1ff.). But Satan "tempts" or tests us to prove us faithless (cf. Job 1-2). As in the case of Job God permits us to be tested in order to prove Satan's slanderous accusations false.

The truth of the matter is that Satan does not tempt us in our baser but in our higher nature. W. Hersey Davis defined sin as "an illegitimate expression of a legitimate desire." Satan strikes at our legitimate *desires* in order to pervert them to his own nefarious ends. Basically he tempts us in our physical appetites, aesthetic nature, and spiritual desire. "And when the woman saw that the tree was good for food [physical appetite], and that it was pleasant to the eyes [aesthetic nature], and a tree to be desired to make one wise [spiritual desire; note "gods" in Gen. 3:5 should read "God," *Elohim,* cf. Gen. 1:1]. . ." (Gen. 3:6). Satan tempted Jesus in the same areas (cf. Matt. 4:3, 6, 9). When Luke 4:13 says that Jesus was tempted in "all the temptation," literally, "every kind of temptation," he means that Jesus was tempted in every area in which it is possible to be tempted. Satan struck at legitimate desires in order to get both Eve and Jesus to give them illegitimate expressions. He succeeded with Eve, but failed with Jesus.

Now when we apply these thoughts to James 1:14-15 what

do we find? After saying that God tempts no man to do evil (v. 13), he says, "But every man is tempted [tested], when he is drawn away of his own lust, and enticed [baited as a fish]. Then when lust hath conceived, it bringeth forth sin: and sin, when it is finished, bringeth forth death."

Note that "lust" appears twice. Both of these translate the word *epithumia*. But there is a difference. In verse 14 it is "his own *epithumia*" (*tēs idias epithumias*). This means the natural *desire* or that which is God-given. But in verse 15 it is simply "the *epithumia*" (*hē epithumia*). It is a desire which is not his own or natural to him. It is the God-given "desire" which has been perverted into "lust."

So this should read literally, "But each one is tested by his own God-given desire being allured and baited as a fish. Then the perverted desire conceiving [in our wills] births sin: and sin having reached full growth produces the abortion of death." That which Satan promised is not a beautiful, living thing; it is death itself (cf. Rom. 6:23).

God gives us *epithumia* to enable us to live the rich and abundant life. When it falls into bad company it ends in death. "Be not deceived: evil communications corrupt good manners" (I Cor. 15:33). Plainly speaking, "You are running with the wrong crowd, and they are corrupting your morals." Do not let your *epithumia* be deceived by the devil!

GUMNAZŌ

(A Spiritual Gymnasium)

This verb connotes *exercise* as in a gymnasium. Athletes usually trained naked (*gumnos*). This verb is derived from this custom. Literally, it means to exercise or train naked. But it came to be used as a metaphor for training the mental and spiritual powers. From it comes the noun, *gumnasia,* which means training or exercise. It is from this word that we derive our word "gymnasium," the place where such exercising was done.

Moulton and Milligan list no papyri example of *gumnasia.* But they cite one inscription which uses the word denoting exercising for the games or athletic contests.

One striking example of *gumnazō* as found in the papyri. It reads, "I had a good bout" with certain *epitropoi* (foremen, stewards, or officers). Whether or not this refers to physical or mental struggle, "bout" (*gumnazō*) gets its flavor from the physical idea. In the sense of a metaphor this word is used by Epictetus in the following sense: "Therefore first upon the spectacle the philosophers exercised us." While not papyri, it does illustrate the example cited above. In like fashion Galen, the physician, uses *gegumnasmena* (perfect passive participle of *gumnazō,* exact form used in Heb. 5:14) in the sense of "I have exercised the organ of perception" or internal sense. And these usages throw light on the New Testament examples of these words.

Gumnazō appears only four times in the New Testament (I Tim. 4:7; Heb. 5:14; 12:11; II Peter 2:14), and *gumnasia* appears only once (I Tim. 4:8).

Paul was fond of drawing on athletic terminology to express spiritual truth (cf. I Cor. 9:24-27). Therefore, his use of both of our words in one passage is not surprising. It is also significant that he employs them to instruct a young man (Timothy) who himself may have been at one time a participant in athletic contests. His Greek heritage on his father's side implies the possibility of such. At any rate as a young man this advice of his elderly father in the faith suggests his understanding of the metaphor.

The full significance of Paul's use of these words is best seen in the contrast of ideas involved. "But refuse profane and old wives' fables, and exercise [*gumazō*] thyself rather unto godliness" (4:7). The contrast is between "old wives' fables," that which would appeal to the aged women, and bodily exercise which is more becoming to a young man. Instead of sitting among the old women indulging in fables, as a young man he is to exercise or train as in a gymnasium in the matters of "faith and good doctrine" (v. 6). The result will be "godliness," the fruit of such training.

Then he points out the superiority of such spiritual exercise over that of the body. "For bodily exercise [hē somatike gumnasia] profiteth little [a little time]: but godliness is profitable unto all things [or for all time], having promise of the life that now is, and of that which is to come" (v. 8). Physical exercise develops only the body which will perish. Spiritual exercise develops the spirit which is eternal. This is a most vital text in a time when such stress is being placed on "physical fitness" alone.

Gumnazō appears twice in Hebrews. It is understandable that an author steeped in the Greek atmosphere of Alexandria would use this word. In Hebrews 5:14 he exhorts those who are babes in Christ to grow up into men who will "have their senses [not muscles] exercised to discern both good and evil." These babes are still drinking "milk," a sign of their immaturity (v. 13). "Strong meat" was the food of athletes even as it is today. The "strong meat" is an advanced comprehension of and exercise in moral principles derived from a thorough knowledge of the Word of God (cf. v. 12). What a text for an age of immature and anemic Christians!

Hebrews 12:11 deals with "chastening" or the discipline used in the training of a child. The fact that one experiences such under God proves his sonship (vv. 8-10). This training may not seem good for the present. But the end result is "the peaceable fruit of righteousness unto them which are exercised [trained as in a gymnasium] thereby" (v. 11). The athlete may not enjoy the rigorous training schedule. But thereby he is enabled to enjoy the fruits of victory. In a sports-minded age such as ours, illustrations of this abound on every hand. What a text for a time of easy living, physically, morally, and spiritually, when the trend of the day is to scorn the rules of righteous living!

In II Peter 2:14 gumnazō is used in an evil sense. Peter is writing to the Jews of the Dispersion (I Peter 1:1, probably the same addressees in II Peter), Jews who lived in the Gentile environment of Asia Minor. They would be familiar with Greek athletics.

But here he speaks of those whose hearts "they have exercised [trained as in a gymnasium] with covetous practices. . . ." They have "eyes full of adultery, and that cannot cease from sin; beguiling unstable souls. . . ." Peter calls them "cursed children." What a text for a generation of delinquent adults and youth!

In all of these examples the New Testament writers use the moral and spiritual metaphor. But it finds its force in the basic meaning of *gumnazō* as exercising and training for physical athletic contests. However, we should remember that athletes train for a contest. It will profit little if Christian athletes train in the gymnasium but never strive in the arena.

HĒLIKIA

(Age)

The papyri has cast great light on the meaning of this word. It appears eight times in the New Testament. Five times in the Authorized Version it is translated "stature" with an occasional marginal reading of "age" (Matt. 6:27; Luke 2:52; 12:25; 19:3; Eph. 4:13). Three times it is rendered as "age" (John 9:21, 23; Heb. 11:11). But the preponderance of evidence in the papyri gives to it the meaning of "age."

According to Moulton and Milligan, Luke 19:3 is the only New Testament passage where it must mean "stature." Otherwise there is no evidence for any meaning other than "age."

In the papyri the word is found often in the sense of one being "under age" or coming "of age." In Egypt this occurred at the age of fourteen years. One example reads "approaching the legal age." Another concerns a man who has reached the age of seventy asking to be relieved from performing certain public duties. Of like fashion is the reading "If you can claim the assistance due to immature age, the praefect of the province shall decide the suit for release." Again, "making for my orphan daughter who is under age." It should be noted, however, that one example (about A.D. 250) is translated by the editors, "Who could add to your stature [*hēlikian*]? He himself will give you your garment." But according to Moulton and Milligan "it must be sufficient to summarize by stating that no one who reads the papyri can have any doubt that the word means 'age' in ordinary parlance."

There is no problem when these thoughts are applied to John 9:21, 23 and Hebrews 11:11. But even here the papyri serves to emphasize the meaning of "age." In the former reference the parents of the man say literally, "He has *hēlikian*, he is of age." In the latter the meaning is "beyond the proper age" (*hēlikias*). These are in harmony with examples cited above.

However, certain problems arise with respect to the other New Testament passages. The context of Luke 19:3 calls for *hēlikia* to be rendered "stature," which is in keeping with the one papyri reference of A.D. 250. Some scholars prefer this rendering for the remaining references. But the weight of evidence both in the papyri and in the Scriptural context seems to favor "age."

For instance, Luke 2:52 says, "And Jesus increased in wisdom and stature, and in favor with God and man." "Increased" renders a word implying effort on the part of Jesus. It means "to cut one's way forward" as one cutting his way through the jungle growth. In "wisdom" and "favor" He cut His way forward by personal application and conduct. Since the word *hēlikia* appears in this context it could mean that by work and other exercise Jesus "cut his way forward" in bodily stature. Or it could mean the natural accretion of years and the maturity which accompanies such. The papyri examples seem to favor "age." But the context would allow either.

Furthermore, in Ephesians 4:13 the meaning of *hēlikia* could be either "stature" or "age." However, in this case the context seems to call for "age." Paul is speaking of maturity as seen in the expression "the perfect man." The word "perfect" renders a word which connotes arriving at a desired goal. Paul is not thinking of the size of an adult man, but of his maturity as reflected in age. He is concerned that his readers shall not act as children, or those not yet of legal age, but as those who have reached the "age" of maturity: "that we henceforth be no more children . . . but speaking the truth in love. . ." (cf. I Cor. 13:11). To be sure if one emphasizes the *body* and the "head" (Eph. 4:15) "stature" could be the meaning. But this is to think of the physical aspects. Paul's meaning seems to run deeper. If so, then "age" seems to be the preferable connotation.

In no place does the papyri assist with this word as in Matthew 6:27 and Luke 12:25. Both say practically the same thing. "Which of you by taking thought can add one cubit unto his stature?" (Matt. 6:27). At first sight "stature" might be appropriate. The word for "cubit" originally meant distance or the length of the forearm (cf. John 21:8; Rev. 21:17). But Arndt and Gingrich cite a reference where this word also means "a cubit of time." Thus in the light of the papyri emphasis on *hēlikia* as "age" they translate these passages "add a single hour to his life."

Furthermore, Moulton and Milligan follow the same trend. They cite with strong approval the *Twentieth Century* translation, "Which of you, by being anxious, can prolong his life a moment." They note further, "That worry *shortens* life is the fact which adds point to the irony. The desire to turn a six-footer into a Goliath is rather a bizarre ambition."

HUIOTHESIA

(Adoption as Sons)

In the New Testament this word appears only in the Pauline writings (Rom. 8:15, 24; 9:4; Gal. 4:5; Eph. 1:5). There was a time when scholars regarded this word as one coined by Paul. But Deissmann has shown that it abounds in inscriptions which antedate New Testament times (e.g., second century B.C.). Examples have been found in papyri dated in the second and fourth centuries A.D. So it is now evident that Paul simply borrowed a word in current usage, and used it to express a great Christian truth. The word itself means the state of being made a son. It is rendered in English as "adoption" from the Latin *adoptio filiorum* (Vulgate).

Two examples of *huiothesia* may be cited from the papyri. An agreement on adoption reads, "we agree, Herachs and his wife Isarion on the one part, that we have given away to you, Horion, for adoption our son Patermouthis, aged about two years, and I Horion on the other part, that I have him as my own son so that the rights proceeding from succession to my inheritance shall be maintained for him." Another reads, "So that with respect to me his brother Silbanon . . . to have for adoption."

In ancient times the custom prevailed whereby one would, under certain conditions, adopt a child not his own which received the rights, privileges, and responsibilities of being one's own child. Three examples of this are found in the Old Testament, where in each instance it was the adoption of a slave (Exod. 2:10; I Kings 11:20; Esth. 2:7, 15). Among the Greeks and Romans the adoptive child might be a slave but was usually a free person or citizen. It would seem that Paul combines the Greek and Roman act of adoption with that of the Hebrew where the adoptive child was a slave. However, if we regard the unsaved as children of Satan, even the other idea is involved also.

Under Roman law, which must have been uppermost in Paul's mind, certain legal steps were prescribed. These were based on the method of the sale of slaves known as mancipation. The vendor and the vendee must be present. In the case of parents the real parents and one doing the adopting must be present. At least five witnesses were required to make the transaction legal. Present also was the one to weigh in scales the money involved. Certain words were exchanged. Then the purchaser or adopting father simulated the payments of money by striking the scales with money. The vendor or real father replied with certain words. The witnesses vouched for the transaction that it had been carried out legally. Thus the adoption was completed.

The adoptive son then became the son of the adopting father. He severed all former ties. In return any debts of the son were cancelled. In the eyes of the law he became a new creature as though he had been born into a new family in which he became an heir of his new father and a joint-heir with naturally born children. He assumed the responsibilities of sonship, and received all of its privileges. All of this is bound up in the meaning of the word *huiothesia*.

One cannot fail to see a relationship between this idea and that contained in the words "born again" (John 3:3). However, they should not be regarded as synonymous. For "born again" is strictly a Hebrew idea involving a new nature. Whereas "adoption" is a Roman idea involving a new relationship. However, in Paul's use of adoption there is a combination of both ideas. We have seen that the Hebrew custom of adoption seems to have involved slaves only, whereas the Roman pertained more to citizens, yet the custom used in the mancipation of slaves was followed. Indeed, even among the Romans slaves were sometimes adopted. But Paul's uses of the word *huiothesia* involved more than a mere legal transaction. The interplay of personalities or natures is quite evident.

Two uses of *huiothesia* by Paul are rather simple, where he speaks of Israel having the "adoption" of sons of God (Rom. 9:4), and of Gentiles having "the adoption of children by Jesus Christ" (Eph. 1:5). But even here the figure holds. However, in Romans 8:15 and Galatians 4:5 the details of the transaction of adoption are seen. Both instances are based upon the idea of slaves being adopted into a family of free men.

In Romans 8 Paul sees those who are enslaved by the law of sin and death (v. 2). They possess "the spirit of bondage" (v. 15). Only those who "are led by the Spirit of God . . . are the sons of God." Thus Paul draws from the custom of *huiothesia* to express the change by which slaves to the law may become free sons of God. By "the law of the Spirit of life in Christ Jesus" (vendee) the slave is freed from "the law of sin and death" (vendor, v. 2). The price paid is that Christ died and "condemned sin in the flesh" (v. 3). Those who receive Him receive the "Spirit of adoption." Thus they become sons of God, crying, "Abba, Father" (v. 15). Note that the Holy Spirit is the one who "beareth witness with our spirit, that we are the children of God" (v. 16). That Paul has in mind both the privileges and responsibilities of sonship is seen in verses 17-18. But the "children of God" do not realize the full meaning of *huiothesia* until the resurrection or the "redemption of the body" (v. 23).

The same detail is seen in Galatians 4. Here the adoptive child is enslaved by the law (v. 5) or "the elements of the world" (v. 3), the vendor. The vendee is God (v. 4). The price paid is seen in the word "redeem" (v. 5). Thereby the slave becomes a son of God by *huiothesia* (v. 5) whereby he cries, "Abba, Father" (v. 6). The Spirit again is seen as the witness (v. 6). The privilege of sonship is expressed in verse 7, and the responsibility of the same appears in verses 8-9.

It should be noted, however, that in both examples the experience is not merely a legal transaction, but one which sets forth the interplay of the persons involved. Thus the message of the New Testament is enhanced by the papyri in one of Paul's greatest illustrations of that which is experienced as slaves to sin become sons of God.

HUPOTITHĒMI

(A Mortgage on One's Neck)

This verb means "to place under." It appears only twice in the New Testament (Rom. 16:4; I Tim. 4:6). In I Timothy 4:6 it is rendered "put in remembrance." And this is not a bad translation. But among the papyri is found a private letter almost contemporary (A.D. 1/2) with Paul which clearly uses this word (middle voice) for *advice*, *suggests*, or to *point out* something to someone, *to teach*. Arndt and Gingrich support these uses, noting that they are also found in classical Greek. The idea of *advise* or *suggest* notes the delicate manner in which "a good minister of Jesus Christ" will deal with problems among his flock.

But in Romans 16:4 the meaning is quite different and most picturesque. Paul speaks of those who have "laid down their own necks" for his life. Deissmann illustrates this thought from the papyri in the statement, "for the most beloved of his relatives or friends he would readily stake his neck." However, the verb used here is *paraballō*, cast alongside. This is more in the sense of sharing one's peril, as one casts his own neck alongside those of others. Paul's expression is stronger. For *hupotithēmi* has the idea of placing one's neck under something on behalf of another's life. This suggests the idea of beheading one with the sword. So to save Paul's life Priscilla and Aquila figuratively placed their own necks under the sword in his place.

In the papyri a more meaningful use is found, that of a

"mortgage." In a will dated A.D. 156, a man says, "My wife shall have the right to sell and mortgage [*hupotithesthai*] on her own authority anything she chooses." A similar use is found for "having the power of sale, mortgage, gift" (A.D. 159). While these postdate Paul by about a century, the meaning is not out of keeping with his figure. His two friends mortgaged their own necks to save his.

This is suggestive of the saying of the greatest Friend. "Greater love hath no man than this, that a man lay down [*thēi* from *tithēmi*] his life for his friends" (John 15:13). Truly Jesus "placed under" or "mortgaged" His own life to save ours in both time and eternity.

KATAKRINŌ

(Guilty!)

This verb is formed with *krinō*, to decide, in the sense of considering two or more things and reaching a decision, (cf. "determined," Acts 20:16; I Cor. 2:2; Titus 3:12), and *kata*, down. So *katakrinō* means to decide down, or to reach a final decision in a matter. *Krinō* and its derivative (*krisis*) may refer to ordinary decisions or those connected with the processes of law (cf. John 3:18-20). *Krisis* is sometimes used of the activity of God or Christ as judge, especially on the Last Day (cf. Matt. 12:41). But *krima* means a condemnatory judgment or sentence (cf. Matt. 7:12; John 9:39; Heb. 6:2). In the papyri this word is never used of a trial which ended in acquittal.

However, *katakrinō* and its derivatives always carry the flavor of legal processes, even when used in the religious sense.

This position is borne out by the papyri. The verb *katakrinō* is used in one such as "but if the case be decided against me." Another deals with a case where property under a mortgage was seized by the creditor, Sempronius Orestinus. The Prefect informs him that if he does not make restitution "not only will he be sentenced but also scourged." So this verb refers to the act of judging and pronouncing sentence.

The noun *katakrisis* connotes the sentence itself. One example speaks of "condemnations for envy." But the noun *katakrima* means the punishment brought on by the sentence. Thus one papyri example speaks of "a judgment" to be paid as a fine or damages. Moulton and Milligan cite several such cases. It follows, therefore, that this word does not mean "condemnation" in the sense of a court verdict, but to the punishment which follows the sentence. According to Moulton and Milligan we are not justified always to distinguish between *krinō* and *katakrinō* and their derivatives. At times the former have a legal sense, and at others a non-legal meaning. The context must decide. But the latter is the stronger family of words (i.e., *kata* adds emphasis), and is always expressive of judgment with a legal flavor.

Applying these thoughts about *katakrinō* to the New Testament usages yields happy results in the finer points of interpretation. For instance, in the Last Judgment (*krisis*) the men of Nineveh and the queen of Sheba "shall rise in judgment with [*meta*] this generation . . ." (Matt. 12:41f.; Luke 11:31f.). "With" is ambiguous here. It could mean "with" in the sense of jointly standing before the judgment seat. Or it could mean "against this generation." Either or both make sense. At the judgment they will prove the guilt of and bring sentence (*katakrinō*) upon those who reject Jesus. Those on trial will themselves be the evidence of a greater guilt upon the unbelievers. Hence the greater sentence. They will not "condemn" in the sense of administering punishment. But they will be the evidence that will decide the issue. In a sense they will pronounce them *guilty*.

A similar usage is seen with respect to Jesus' "condemnation" (Matt. 20:18; 27:3; Mark 10:33; 14:64). In each of these references "condemned" should read "found guilty and pronounced sentence." They did not carry out the sentence; this was done by others.

In the story of the woman taken in adultery this word appears twice (John 8:10f.). There was no question of the woman's guilt since she had been caught in the act. Her accusers quoted the Mosaic law as to her punishment. Jesus challenged anyone among them without sin to cast the first stone. One by one the men slipped away. Asking as to her accusers, Jesus said, ". . .hath no man condemned thee?" (*katakrinō*). Here the meaning is "hath no man pronounced sentence [stoning] upon you?" Then He said, "Neither do I pronounce sentence upon you." Note that this has no reference to her guilt, but to the sentence of stoning. With an admonition toward righteousness Jesus sent her away unharmed.

A very striking picture is seen in Romans 2:1. When one sinner judges another, he ["condemnest," *katakrinō*] finds himself guilty and pronounces the same sentence upon himself. In Romans 14:23 the one judging between ("doubteth") meats, if he eats meat "has been found guilty and sentence pronounced" ("is damned"), because of his conviction against such. God chastens His children that they may not be *found guilty and sentenced* along with the world (I Cor. 11:32). By Noah's faith and obedience he became the basis of conviction and sentence upon his own generation (Heb. 11:7). James 5:9 reads, ". . . lest ye be found guilty and sentenced . . ." In II Peter 2:6 the guilt, sentence, and punishment are all involved.

Two examples of *katakrisis* appear in the New Testament. In II Corinthians 3:9 Paul contrasts the Mosaic law with the "new testament" (v. 6). Implied is the thought that the law is a "ministration of the pronounced sentence of death." In II Corinthians 7:3 Paul says literally "to pronounce sentence I am not speaking."

In Romans 5:16, 18 the word for "condemnation" is *katakrima,* the punishment resulting from the sentence. Literally, ". . . for the condemnatory sentence [*krima*] was out of one [Adam] unto a punishment prescribed by the sentence. . ." (cf. 5:18).

Perhaps one of the richest uses of *katakrinō* and *katakrima* is found in Romans 8. In verse 1 "condemnation" is *kata-krima*, the punishment prescribed by the sentence after one is found guilty. Those in Christ shall not suffer such. For God in Christ "condemned [pronounced guilty and sentenced] sin in the flesh" (v. 3). This sentence was carried out in the *katakrima* which Jesus suffered on the cross. In so doing God justified or declared righteous those who believe in Christ (v. 33). "Who is he that finds [us] guilty and pronounces sentence [*katakrinō*]? It is Christ that died . . . that is risen again, who is even at the right hand of God, who also maketh intercession for us" (v. 34).

This is the gospel indeed. Found guilty and sentenced of God to die for our sins, yet God by His grace put our guilt upon His Son. The Son suffered the results of the sentence. So for those in Him there is no suffering under the sentence of death. Nothing shall "separate us from the love of God, which is in Christ Jesus our Lord" (cf. vv. 38-39).

Truly Jesus became all that we are that we might become all that He is (Rom. 8:1-4, 34).

KOINŌNEŌ

(The Tie That Binds)

This verb and its derivatives form one of the most blessed families in the Christian vocabulary. It means to share or to have a share in common with someone in something. Thus its basic thought is to have fellowship or partnership. One form of this word (*koinōnikos*) describes the Christian's attitude to "communicate" or share his goods with others (I Tim. 6:18). The noun *koinōnos* refers to the one sharing and so a partner (cf. Luke 5:10). Another noun *koinōnia* speaks of the experience of sharing itself (cf. Phil. 1:5).

These meanings are amply illustrated in the papyri. One example of *koinōneō* speaks of those who shelter criminals as "being partners in their misdeeds." A touching example is an inscription which a doctor has inscribed to his wife, who herself had studied medicine, reading, "as with you alone I shared my life." Although not from the papyri, it shows the usage.

These meanings carry over into the New Testament. It speaks of those who are partners in sin (I Tim. 6:22; II John 11). Since the Hebrew Christians *shared* the gospel with the Gentiles ("partakers"), they in turn should *be partners* in sharing with them their goods (Rom. 15:27; cf. 12:13, "distributing," this verb). These suggest the offering by Gentile churches for the persecuted Hebrew Christians of Palestine (cf. Rom. 15:25ff.; I Cor. 16:1ff.; II Cor. 8-9; Acts 20:4). The Philippian church "communicated with" or shared money as a gift to Paul (Phil. 4:15). As men are "partners" or partners in human nature, so Christ became the same (Heb. 2:14). And when the Christians suffer persecution they have a partnership with Christ in His sufferings (prior to the cross) (I Peter 4:13).

Koinōnikos is used in the sense of land being "common" to two properties. Thus it bears the nature of being shared by two owners. In the Christian sense possession and need produce a common ground or partnership. Thus the possessor should communicate to the one in need (cf. I Tim. 6:18). This is not forced communism but voluntary Christian *koinōnia* (cf. Acts 4:34ff.).

Koinōnos is used in the papyri as partner. In a fishing contract one Hermes takes Cornelius as his "partner" to the extent of a sixth share in the annual rent of a lake. A father writes to his son, "Our partner has taken no share in the work." Still further, " I will have no partner or servant who is liable on account of the contract."

In each New Testament use of this word the idea of "partners" is present. Three times it is so translated (Luke 5:10; II Cor. 8:23; Philem. 17). But all other examples may also be so rendered. The Jews say that they would not have been "partners" with their fathers in slaying the prophets (Matt. 23:30). In Hebrew ritual those eating the sacrifice became "partners" of the altar or with the sacrifice (I Cor. 10:18). In like fashion Christians are not to participate in pagan sacrifices and thus become "partners" with devils (I Cor. 10:20). "Partners" of the sufferings may become the same in consolation (II Cor. 1:7). "Companions" in Hebrews 10:33 carries the same idea. Peter says that as he was a witness of the sufferings of Christ, so shall he be a "partner" with respect to His glory in heaven (I Peter 5:1). And by the promises of God we all may become "partners" in the divine nature (II Peter 1:4).

But the richest of all these words is *koinōnia*. It expresses the closest of all human relationships. In the papyri in the time of Augustus Caesar it is used in a marriage contract, implying the greatest of intimacy, love, and sharing. One example renders it "belonging in common to." In the business sense it occurs in the statement "my brother on my father's side, with whom I have no *partnership*" (author's italics). One very striking usage is found in Epictetus (not papyri) which depicts one's union with deity: "aiming to have fellowship with Zeus."

In the New Testament *koinōnia* expresses the close relationship which characterizes Christian "fellowship" (cf. Acts 2:42). In Romans 15:26 it is rendered "contribution," or the sharing of Gentile churches with the poor saints in Jerusalem (cf. also II Cor. 8:4, "fellowship," 9:13, "distribution"; Phil. 1:5, "fellowship;" note the verb in Phil. 4:15, "communicate"). All of these foregoing references involved the sharing of money. They speak of the care which one Christian should have for all other Christians. The Philippian references are great missionary texts challenging us to have "fellowship" in the gospel.

A sharing of missionary responsibility is seen in Galatians 2:9. "The right hands of fellowship" imply not only the healing of a breach between Christians, but a pledge of partnership in the various phases of missionary work (cf. Heb. 13:16; Philem. 6, "communicate").

A most interesting study is found in II Corinthians 6:14-15. Three different words are used to express the same idea. "What fellowship [*metochē*, meaning partnership, cognate of *koinōnia*] hath righteousness with unrighteousness? and what communion [*koinōnia*] hath light with darkness? and what concord [*sumphōnēsis*, symphony] hath Christ with Belial?" The Christian should never be in *koinōnia* with anything or anyone outside of Christ. This lesson drawn from a marriage with unbelievers is enhanced by the papyri example of marriage as a *koinōnia*.

This word is also used for the intimacy of the Christians' relationship in and with the Lord (cf. Epictetus' example of Zeus). Ephesians 3:9 speaks of the *koinōnia* of the "mystery" whereby God will make both Jew and Gentile one in Christ (cf. Gal. 3:26-39; Eph. 2:11-22). It denotes the intimate union of the Christian with Christ (Phil. 3:10) and with the Holy Spirit (Phil. 2:1). This "communion" or fellowship with Christ is symbolically expressed in the ordinance of the Lord's Supper (I Cor. 10:16).

The *koinōnia* among Christian people is based upon their *koinōnia* with "the Father, and with his Son Jesus Christ" (I John 1:3). Our inner *koinōnia* with God is proved or disproved by our outward life (I John 1:6). "If we walk in the light, as he is in the light, we have *koinōnia* one with another, and the blood of Jesus Christ his Son cleanseth us from all sin" (I John 1:7).

Blessed tie that binds us not only to God in Christ, but to all who are in Christ!

KURIAKOS

(Paganism or Christianity?)

This is an adjective derived from the word *kurios*, which means "lord" or when it refers to deity, "Lord." In some instances *kurios* may be rendered "master," "owner," "sir" (a title of respect). In one case it is translated "God" (Acts 19:20). Six hundred and sixty-seven times in the New Testament it is rendered "Lord."

In secular life *kurios* was used to refer to any person of high position, even as in some countries today it is used of royalty or a titled person. It was used especially of the Roman emperors, sometimes in the sense of deity. Inscriptions abound to this effect. The adjective *kuriakos* should be translated "lordly."

Until Deissmann's discovery that the Greek of the New Testament is identical with that of the papyri, *kuriakos* was considered to be purely a Biblical or ecclesiastical word. But now we know that this was a word common to the language of the people, and which was employed in the New Testament to express great Christian truths.

In the papyri *kuriakos* is rendered "Imperial." A camel is provided "for Imperial caravans that travel from Bernice." It is used in such references as "Imperial ownership," "Imperial treasury," "Imperial revenue," and "for the Imperial service in Syria."

Deissmann cites one inscription (not papyri) where the name *Sebaste* (Augustus) is found in denoting "Emperor's Day." This is most significant with reference to Revelation 1:10.

Revelation 1:10 is one of two places in the New Testament

where *kuriakos* is found. John says, "I was in the Spirit on the Lord's Day" (*en tēi kuriakēi hēmerai*). The "Lord's day" is interpreted to mean Sunday, even as the word *kuriakē* in modern Greek means *Sunday*. This was the "first day of the week" (Matt. 28:1; I Cor. 16:2).

The "first day of the week" is the Christian day set aside for worship, as the "seventh day" was used in the old dispensation. The word "Sabbath" means "rest." It commemorated God's "rest" from His act of creation. The "first day of the week" commemorates the Lord's "rest" from His redemptive act (i.e., the resurrection). In the New Testament after the resurrection of Jesus Christians are not found, as Christians, worshipping on the seventh day. Paul and others went into the synagogues on that day, because they found a ready-made audience. But when Christians as such gathered for worship it was on the "first day of the week" (cf. Acts 20:7ff.; I Cor. 16:1ff.). Hence this came to be called "the Lord's day" (Rev. 1:10).

But does not the inscription cited above suggest another reason for calling the "first day" the "Lord's day?" In protest against the pagan custom of observing a *kuriakos day* or "Emperor's Day" in honor of Emperor Augustus, the Christians called their day of worship a *kuriakos day* or "Lordly Day." Thus we see that this day is a contrast with both the Jewish Sabbath and the Roman "Emperor's Day." It sets forth Christianity as distinct in a world of many religions.

The other use of *kuriakos* is found in I Corinthians 11:20. Paul is dealing with problems growing out of abuses connected with the *Agape*, a love feast observed by early Christians, and the observance of the Last Supper which followed. The participants brought their own food for the *Agape*. Some had much; others had little. This served to produce a cleavage in the fellowship of the church. It appears that some even became intoxicated (I Cor. 11:21). Robertson and Plummer comment on this: "Hungry poor meeting intoxicated rich, at what was supposed to be a supper of the Lord."

Paul comments on this. " When ye come together therefore into one place, this is not to eat the Lord's Supper" (*kuriakon deipnon*, I Cor. 11:20). Some see "Lord's supper" as the "Last Supper" or what we call the *Lord's Supper*. However, this makes Paul say what he did not intend to say. They did come together to partake of the *Lord's Supper*. The problem was their abuse of this purpose.

The papyri serves to clear up this matter. "Lord's supper" (11:20) is a "lordly supper" or "Imperial supper." The pagan feasts in honor of the emperor were bacchanalian banquets characterized by gorging and drunkenness. So Paul is saying that the Corinthian Christians did not come together to eat a pagan "Imperial supper" but a "Supper of the Lord." Thus Paul issues a stinging rebuke to these Christians for acting like pagans at a time when they should be most Christlike. Note that "unworthily" in I Corinthians 11:27, 29 refers to this *pagan* practice being indulged in by these Christians. It is not an adjective as some think, but an adverb of manner. It speaks of the manner in which they were observing the Last Supper, not to personal character.

Of interest also are the words "when ye come together therefore in one place" in their relation to *kuriakos*. At this time they had no church buildings, but assembled for worship in some Christian's home. It was not until about the fourth century A.D. that they had church buildings in which to worship. Thus we note with interest that a fourth century papyri example reads, "When I had gone out to the church at Sambatho." The English word "church" in the sense of a church building comes from the word *kuriakos*. Thus a church building is a "lordly house" or "the Lord's house."

LOGIZOMAI

(Entered in the Ledger)

In its basic sense this verb is a bookkeeping term. It means to reckon, calculate, or to count or account. It is sometimes used in the sense of crediting something as to an account. It came to suggest reasoning in the sense of considering or evaluating something and so to reach a decision. But in any case its background is that of entering a matter in the ledger after reaching a decision concerning it.

This idea is abundantly illustrated in the papyri. One example reads, "the due amounts in money and corn are *reckoned* here" (author's italics here and following). Again, "let my revenues *be placed on deposit* at the storehouse." It is used in the sense of setting a price on something: *"reckoning* the wine to him at sixteen drachmae the monochore"; "a single artaba, *being reckoned* at one hundred and eighty myriads of denarii." A very striking example reads, "I now give orders generally with regard to all payments made or *credited* to the government." Moulton and Milligan note that from this usage comes the noun *logistērion*, "finance-office." In a more general sense the verb means "number" or to "class amongst." Thus "one foal being now *numbered* among the full-grown (camels)." Akin to this is the act of considering so as to reach a decision. One very fine example of this reads, "For who is so utterly wanting in reason and the capacity for *making decisions?"*

These composite ideas carry over into Modern Greek in two words: *logiazō*, consider, think upon; *logarizō*, reckon, value.

The first example of this word in the New Testament implies *considering* a matter but failing to reach a decision

(Mark 11:31ff.). More in keeping with the idea of bookkeeping is Mark 15:28. "And he was numbered with the transgressors" (cf. Luke 22:37, reckoned). He was listed or entered into the accounts as such. The idea of a debit is seen in Acts 19:27 where the temple of Artemis is in danger of being *despised* or entered into the accounts as nothing. This same thought is present in II Timothy 4:16 where Paul prays that his being forsaken by others "may not be laid to their charge" as a debit against them as sin. Also this thought may be seen in passages regarding God *imputing* or *reckoning* sin or unrighteousness to one (Rom. 4:8; II Cor. 5:19).

Conversely this word is used of God crediting the believer's account with "righteousness." The idea is that this word is written across the entire account, thus canceling the entire debt of sin written against one. This word "righteousness" (*dikaiosunē*) belongs to a family of nouns ending in "ē" which mean that a condition is not necessarily true, but which God chooses to regard as true. In Romans it speaks not of an attribute of God but of His gracious activity whereby He picks one up out of the wrong and puts him down in the right as though he had never been in the wrong. This is a favorite word of Paul (used 60 times, 36 in Romans). It is more meaningful than "remission," which speaks of sins committed but forgiven. "Righteousness" means that God looks on us "in Christ" as though we had never sinned.

It is clear, therefore, that this word carried a judicial sense wherein God the just Judge, in Christ becomes also the Justifier of him that believeth in Jesus (cf. Rom. 3:26). So when this word is used with *logizomai* it is in the sense of business law.

In this sense we may read Romans 4:3 "Abraham believed God, and it was counted unto him [put down to his account] for righteousness." This accounting is by grace through faith apart from works. If one hopes to achieve it by works, it is "reckoned" [*logizomai*] not "of grace, but of debt" (4:4), a debt which he cannot pay. It remains on God's books as a debit. But to those who do not depend on works, "but believeth on him that justifieth [righteousness] the ungodly, his

faith is counted [put down to his credit] for righteousness"
(4:5). This same thought is involved in such works as "im-
pute" (4:6, 8, 11, 22-24; cf. Gal. 3:6; James 2:23), "reckon"
(4:9, 10), and "count" (Rom. 2:26).

In Romans 8:36 Paul says of his sufferings for the gospel
that he is entered into the books along with sheep which are
listed for slaughter. Even in such uses as "think" (Rom. 2:3;
I Cor. 13:11; II Cor. 3:5; 10:2, 7, 11; 12:6), "conclude" (Rom.
3:28), "reckon" (Rom. 6:11; 8:18), "count" (Rom. 9:8; Phil.
3:13), "account" (I Cor. 4:1; Heb. 11:19), "suppose" (II Cor.
11:5; I Peter 5:12), "esteem" (Rom. 14:14), and "think on"
(Phil. 4:8) the sense involves the weighing of the evidence and
the entering of the conclusion in the books of the mind or
heart.

One use of this verb where it is rendered "think" is of particular interest. "Thinketh no evil" (I Cor. 13:5). Literally,
"Christian love [*agapē*] . . . does not keep books on the evil"
done against it. This is suggestive of the gracious love of God
in Christ which should find a like expression in the heart of
every Christian.

How is your account with God (cf. Matt. 25:31ff.; Rom.
14:10ff.; Rev. 20:11ff.)? And with man (cf. Matt. 18:23ff.; I
Cor. 13:5)?

LOUŌ, NIPTŌ

(Washed or Rinsed?)

These are two related words and yet quite different. Together with *plunō* they form a triad of words meaning respectively, to bathe the whole body (*louō*), to bathe or rinse
any part of the body (*niptō*), and to wash an article such as
clothes (*plunō*, cf. Luke 5:2; Rev. 7:14). All three words ap-

pear in Leviticus 15:11 (Septuagint). All three words appear in the papyri.

Louō is found in one example as "the *bath* used for the purpose of bathing." In the sense of bathing oneself (middle voice) the word is quite common. One such dated 221 B.C. speaks of a husband urging his wife to return home, stating, "Since we bathed together on Phaophi 12, I never bathed nor anointed myself until Athur 12." This word is found frequently in the sense of religious ceremonial baths.

These usages are borne out in the New Testament. Acts 9:37 speaks of bathing a corpse before laying it out. In Acts 16:33 the Philippian jailer "washed" the stripes of Paul and Silas, suggesting a thorough cleansing, perhaps of the entire body. This suggests the extent of the beatings which they received. Hebrews 10:22 draws on the ceremonial idea in *louō,* "and our bodies washed with pure water." This does not involve baptismal regeneration any more than "hearts sprinkled from an evil conscience" means a literal sprinkling of the heart. It is a figure drawn from the Jewish *ablution* as a ceremonial cleansing, and which is borne out in the papyri. If the author had had baptism in mind he could have used *baptizō,* to submerge or immerse.

In Revelation 1:5 *louō* is used of the believer being "washed from our sins in his own blood." Of course, this does not mean an actual bath in blood. It is a figure of being cleansed from sin, and implies a cleansing of the whole person or soul. There would seem also to be an implied contrast between the thought in *louō,* to bathe the entire body, and *rantizō,* to sprinkle as blood on the mercy seat. The contrast would be between a complete, permanent, and a partial, temporary cleansing.

Moulton and Milligan, following Clemen *Primitive Christianity,* and in the light of the papyri, suggest that II Peter 5:22 should be rendered, ". . . the sow that washes itself by wallowing in the mire."

Moulton and Milligan list only one example of *niptō,* and that from the apocryphal Gospel of Peter. But it is significant to establish the thought of *niptō* referring to a washing of parts of the body, not the whole. It reads, "of the Jews did not wash the hands." This is in contrast to Pilate's ceremonial act of washing his hands. Swete remarks, "The callousness of the Jewish leaders is sharply contrasted with the scruples of the Gentile Procurator." Those who ceremonially washed or rinsed their hands on so many occasions to ward off evil, did not do so on the occasion of their greatest sin.

In the New Testament the washing of only a part of the body is seen in Matthew 6:17. This same thought in the cere-monial sense is found in Matthew 15:2 (cf. Mark 7:3). This does not refer to bodily cleanliness. The idea back of this ritual was that demons got on the hands, and entered the body through the mouth if one ate with unwashed hands.

With one exception (I Tim. 5:1) the remainder of the New Testament examples are found in John. In 9:7, 11, 15 *niptō* is used of the blind man washing in the pool of Siloam. He did not take a bath in the pool, but washed his eyes. The man not only washed the clay from his eyes. Involved also is the ceremonial idea or an act of faith whereby he was cured or cleansed of blindness.

In John 13 there is a marvelous play on the words *louō* and *niptō*. In Jesus' day men wore open sandals. Even though one bathed (*louō*) before departing to another's home, walk-ing on the dusty roads or paths one's feet gathered dust. The host usually had a servant at his door with a basin-of water and a towel with which to rinse the dust from his guests' feet. Since Jesus had no such servant He assumed this role Himself as the *host* at the paschal meal and Last Supper. Thus He taught a lesson in humility and service (cf. I Tim. 5:10).

First, He took a towel and "bason" filled with water. This "bason" is a *niptēr,* wash basin from *niptō*. Then He began to "wash" or rinse (*niptō*) the disciples' feet (v. 5). When He came to Peter, he asked, "Lord, dost thou rinse (*niptō*) my feet?" (v. 6). He remonstrated, "Thou shalt never [unto the ages] rinse my feet" (v. 8). Jesus replied, "If I do not rinse (*niptō*) you, you have no part with me" (v. 8).

Then in his customary fashion Peter replied, "Lord, not my feet only, but also my hands and my head" (v. 9). While he did not use the word, this implied *louō*. In effect, Peter said, "Lord, give me a bath! Wash me all over!" A note of humor may be seen at this point when Jesus took up the implied word. "The one having taken a bath [*leloumenos,* perfect passive participle, suggesting a thorough bathing] has no need except to rinse [*niptō*] the feet." Arndt and Gingrich, following certain classic Greek writers, render *leloumenos* as "newly bathed, after the bath."

In verses 10-13 John notes the mystical meaning of this act. Those who are thoroughly washed in the blood of the Lamb (cf. Rev. 1:5) need only to be *rinsed* in the day to day forgiveness of sins (cf. I John 1:7, 9).

Some hold that John 13:14 teaches a continuing ordinance in feet washing (cf. I Tim. 5:10). However, an ordinance is that which Jesus commanded, and which symbolizes what Jesus did for our salvation: baptism (death, burial, and resurrection of Jesus; cf. also Rom. 6:3-5); Lord's Supper (His broken body and shed blood). John 13:14 is simply an admonition to humble service on behalf of others (cf. I Tim. 5:10).

MARTUREŌ

(I Am a Witness)

This is one of the commoner words in the New Testament. *Martureō* and its derivatives appear one hundred and seventy-three times: *martureō* "I am a witness" or "I witness," 79; *marturia,* testimony or evidence, 37; *marturion,* that which serves as testimony or evidence, 20; *marturomai,* called to testify, 3; *martus,* a witness, 34. Obviously we cannot treat all of these. But an examination of these words in the papyri will shed light on the idea of *witnessing* as found so abundantly in the New Testament.

In the papyri the basic idea of *martureō* is that of giving legal testimony of what one has seen or experienced. It was a common practice to write this word after a signature in the sense that we write "witness." For instance, a will is so witnessed: "I, Serapion, am witness" (*Serapiōn marturō*). The same is found on records of sales and receipts. This word had a judicial usage as seen in "Stotoetis stated that there were present persons able to witness to the murder." Numerous examples appear in the sense of "bear witness to" or "report."

The word *marturia* is used in the sense of "evidence" or "to give evidence": "wherefore I present this petition, requesting that it may be registered as evidence." *Marturion* is found on an inscription in the phrase "the witness of an upright life." One papyri usage refers to a martyr's shrine: "opposite the martyr's shrine." *Marturomai* is found in the sense of being summoned to witness: "called to witness the persons about to seal the present affidavit." This word is also found for *swearing* as in court. *Martus* is used often in the sense of a "witness" to a contract or legal document. A "witness" must be able to give first-hand testimony (cf. Acts 1:22).

So the sense of the word "witness" or "testimony" in the papyri is that of giving evidence as to what one has seen or experienced. It is not hearsay evidence but personal knowledge or experience. And this is significant as to the New Testament meaning of these words.

In Matthew 23:31 *martureō* is used in the sense of self-condemnation. Jesus had just inferred the Pharisees' words by which they disclaimed any guilt with their fathers in the death of the prophets (v. 30). In effect He said that they now write "I am witness (*martureō*) at the end of the statement that they are the children of those who killed the prophets (cf. Luke 11:48).

The word *martureō* appears in John's writings forty-seven times: Gospel, 33; Epistles, 11; Revelation, 3. Six times it is used of John the Baptist concerning Christ (1:7, 8, 15; 3:26; 5:32-33). In John 3:28 John himself calls on his disciples to sign "I am witness" after his words "I am not the Christ, but that I am sent before him." In John 5:31 Jesus says that He cannot "be witness" as proof of His deity, but His works and His Father authenticate His claim (5:36f.; 10:25). Furthermore the Scriptures do the same (5:39).

But in John 8:17-18 Jesus cites the Jewish law requiring two witnesses as evidence (*marturia*), and then names both Himself and His Father as fulfilling the legal requirements.

In John 15:27 we see *martureō* as applied to the disciples. Since they have been with Jesus from the beginning (first-hand knowledge), they can sign their names, "I am witness," to His ministry and teachings. In John 18:23 Jesus challenges the Sanhedrin to give legal proof of their charges against Him. And in 18:37 He tells Pilate that He came to sign His name, "I, Jesus, am witness," to the truth.

An interesting combination appears in John 3:11 where Jesus tells Nicodemus that He has signed, "I, Jesus, am witness" to the truth, but Nicodemus does not receive or accept the "evidence" (*marturian*). The same combination is seen in John 3:32. The one who accepts the "evidence" (*marturian*) knows that God is true (v. 33).

In John 1:32, 34 John the Baptist signs his name, "I am witness" to the statement that Jesus is the Son of God ("bear record," *martureō;* cf. John 8:13f.). Likewise in 4:39 the Samaritan woman signed her name as evidence that He was the Messiah. Jesus Himself signed His name to the statement that a prophet is not without honor save in his own country. (Of course *signing* is not to be taken literally. The thought is in the word *martureō*.)

A most striking combination of *martureō* and *marturia* is found in John 21:24. It would seem that a group of disciples, the Ephesian elders (?), appended this statement to John's Gospel. It is in keeping with the custom of signing a statement (note the papyri examples of witnessing an affidavit) to authenticate evidence. Literally this verse reads, "This is the disciple, the one giving eyewitness testimony of these things, and the one who wrote these things: and we know that his evidence is true." In essence the verse means "We, the Ephesian elders, are witnesses." Incidentally, this verse is strong evidence for the Johannine authorship of the Fourth Gospel.

Several instances of *marturia* have been noted. Additional ones may be cited. The Sanhedrin sought "evidence against Jesus to put him to death; and found none" (Mark 14:55; cf. vv. 56, 59). When Jesus under oath ("adjure," Matt. 26:63) admitted that He was the Son of God, the Sanhedrin said, "What need we any further evidence: for we ourselves have heard of his own mouth" (Luke 22:71).

In I Timothy 3:7 Paul says that the "report" (evidence) of a man's life among non-Christians must be good to qualify him as a bishop. In Titus 1:13 he affirms as true the "evidence" that the Cretans are "liars. . . ." I John 5:9 says that we accept the "evidence" of men (in court). Should we not, therefore, accept God's "greater evidence" which He has "witnessed" (testified, *martureō*) concerning His Son? Furthermore, the one believing in the Son of God has the "evidence" in himself (v. 10). Verses 10-11 use "record" (*marturia*), the recorded evidence. In III John 12 the apostle signs his name ("I, John, am witness," *martureō*) to the good character reference concerning Demetrius, affirming that the "recorded evidence" (*marturia*) is true. In Revelation 1:2 John "bare record" (*emarturēsen*) of the "evidence" (*marturian*) of Jesus Christ "that he saw" (cf. Rev. 1:9; 6:9; 11:7; 12:11, 17; 19:10; 20:4).

A good example of *marturion,* that which serves as evidence, is seen in Matthew 8:4. The healed leper was to show himself to the priest as such (cf. Mark 1:44; Luke 5:14). The legal sense of this word is found in Matthew 10:18 (cf. Mark 13:9; Luke 21:13). The gospel will serve as evidence to all nations (24:14). The disciples are to shake off the dust of any place which rejects their message as the record of evidence against it (Mark 6:11; cf. Luke 9:5). The apostles preached that which served as evidence of the Lord's resurrection (Acts 4:33). When the Lord returns He will be gladly received by those who have believed the record which serves as testimony about Him (II Thess. 1:10). For further study of *marturion* see I Corinthians 1:6; 2:1; II Corinthians 1:12; I Timothy 2:6 ("to be testified" is "the *marturion* in his own time"); II Timothy 1:8; Hebrews 3:5; James 5:3; and Revelation 15:5. In each of these the meaning of *marturion* is flavored with the thought of *that which serves as evidence.*

The word *martus* is generally translated "witness" (cf. Matt. 18:16; 26:65; Acts 1:8; II Tim. 2:2), in the sense of one who bears testimony or gives evidence. In Acts 22:20 and Revelation 2:13; 17:6, it is rendered "martyr" or one who laid down his life as evidence of his faithfulness to Jesus. In II Corinthians 1:23 Paul calls God to the witness stand for a "record" (*martus*) as to his intentions (cf. Phil. 1:8).

An interesting example of this word is found in I Corinthians 15:15. Here Paul combines *martus* with *pseudo* (false), *pseudomartures.* If the dead rise not Paul says that all who have signed their names (*martureō*, testified) to the record of Christ's resurrection are *pseudomartures*, "false witnesses of God." "Of God" can mean either "in God's service" or "concerning God." Either makes sense.

In Acts 20:26 *marturomai* appears in the true papyri sense of calling one to the witness stand. Here Paul calls the Ephesian elders to the witness stand to give evidence that he has wronged no man, and because he has faithfully declared the message of God the blood of no man is on his hands or soul (v. 27). In the other New Testament usages of this word, in the light of the papyri usage of "swearing" in court, the sense seems to be that under oath Paul declares these things to be true (Gal. 5:3; Eph. 4:17).

A great and glorious family of words! But an even greater and weightier responsibility!

MERIMNAŌ, MERIMNA

(Dividing the Mind)

Merimnaō is the verb translated "take no thought" in the King James Version (cf. Matt. 6:25, 27-28, 31, 34). This was a good translation in that day, but is a very poor one today. It suggests irresponsibility for the future. But in old English it taught the very opposite. A. T. Robertson cites a quotation from Bacon (Henry VII): "Harris, an alderman of London, was put in trouble and died with *thought* and anguish" (author's italics). This suggests *anxiety*. Which is a good translation of *merimna*.

In the papyri *merimnaō* is used in the sense of "over-anxiety." One example reads, "I am now writing in haste to prevent your being anxious, for I will see that you are not troubled." Another usage employs *merimna* with the *alpha privative* (*amerimnian*): "For your security [peace of mind] I have issued to you this contract." This same form is found on an inscription as part of a proper name, "*Titedios Amerimnos.*" Ramsey suggests that this may be a baptismal name when Titedios became a Christian, denoting that he is a man who "takes no thought for the morrow" (cf. Matt. 6:34). The word *merimna* is found in a medical sense where one usage is "If the next [toe quiver], he will be involved in much anxiety [*merimnais*] and distress: pray to Zeus."

We can best understand these usages and those in the New Testament by noting that the basic word *merimna*, from which comes the verb *merimnaō*, really means a dividing of the mind. It is a combination form derived from *merizein ton noun*, to divide the mind. It suggests the idea of distraction, or, in some instances in a good sense, of care or concern about one.

89

In this latter sense *merimna* is used for Paul's "care of all the churches" (II Cor. 11:28). In Philippians 2:20 th:s same sense is found in the verb. Paul says that Timothy has the same "care" for the Philippian Christians.

In I Corinthians 7:32-34 we find a combination of both *care* or concern and *distraction*. Speaking of marriage Paul does not wish that the Corinthians shall be *divided in their minds* ("without carefulness," v. 32). In verses 32-34 he contrasts unmarried and married people as those who have an undivided mind toward the things of the Lord and those who are distracted between the things of the Lord (implied) and the interests of their mates respectively. The idea of distraction is implied (schism) as over against mutual concern for one another (I Cor. 12:25).

However, the thought of distraction or divided interests is seen in Luke 10:41. Martha's mind was divided over many things. It would seem that she was anxious about serving a big meal (cf. v. 40), perhaps wondering which dishes to serve, when Jesus said that only one dish was necessary. This is also the sense in Matthew 10:19. When the disciples are brought into court they are not to be overly anxious as to what to say (cf. Luke 12:11).

Perhaps the clearest use of *merimnaō* as distraction is found in Matthew 6:25, 27-28, 31, 34 (cf. Luke 12:22, 25-26). Jesus has just said that "no man can be a slave [*douleuō*] to two masters . . . . ye cannot be a slave to God and mammon" (6:24). "Mammon" is a Chaldean word for the money-god or devil. It is expressive of all that pertains to a worldly view of life.

"Therefore [because, of v. 24] . . . take no thought for your life. . ." (v. 25). "Take no thought" renders *merimnaō*, to be divided in your mind between the things of God and the things of mammon. "Life" is *psuchē*, which here refers to the principle of animal life which indwells both man and beast. The body (*sōma*) must have food, drink, and clothing. But concern over these things are not to divide the mind or loyalty. The Christian owes absolute loyalty to God. The world demands the same. To endeavor to give absolute loyalty to both is to be distracted or divided in mind. This thought is reinforced by the example of fowls and flowers (v. 28). Birds are not idle, neither are they overly anxious. Lilies grow, but from within. We are not to be overly anxious about food and clothing so as to be divided in mind as to our loyalty to God (v. 31). Man is not to live at the animal level (*psuchē*). He is both body (*sōma*), soul (*psuchē*), and spirit (*pneuma*). Indeed, he is not a body which has a spirit. He is a spirit which has a body. His mind should not be divided between the two. It should be united in a proper care of both. Thus he will not be a *split personality* but a well-rounded one.

Nor are we to be distracted about the future (v. 34). The future has its distractions, but we are to live by faith one day at a time. "Sufficient unto the day is the evil thereof" (v. 34). We have trouble enough today without worrying about tomorrow.

A very significant use of *merimnaō* is seen in 6:27. "Stature" may mean height of body or length of days (see *Hēlikia*). Here it probably means length of days. Therefore, a more likely reading is "Which of you by being overly anxious [distracted, divided in your mind] can add one moment to your life?" Worry does not lengthen life. It shortens it. This is a most fitting text for an age of stomach ulcers.

This same thought of distraction is found in Mathew 13:22 (cf. Mark 4:19; Luke 8:14). "Cares" is *merimna*, a divided mind. How such destroys the usefulness of Christian lives!

What is the answer to such a condition? It is found in Philippians 4:6, "Be careful [*merimnaō*] for nothing; but in every thing by prayer and supplication with thanksgiving let your requests be made known unto God." Prayer is the cure of a divided mind.

METOCHOS

(Partnership)

This word comes from the compound Greek verb *metechō*. It is composed of *meta* whose basic meaning is "with" in the sense of being with, among, or in the company of another; and *echō*, to have or to hold. So *metechō* means to have or hold with another as in a joint participation or partnership.

This verb is found in both the inscriptions and the papyri. One inscription associates it with the verb *koinōneō* which means to share or to have a share in something. From this word comes the word which in English is translated "fellowship." Moulton and Milligan note that in this inscription these words *metechō* and *koinōneō* are synonymous (cf. I Cor. 10:17).

This same relationship is seen in one papyri example. ". . . there are many methods of giving them (viz: robbers) shelter: some do so because they are partners [*koinōnountes*] in their misdeeds, others without sharing [*metechontes*] in these yet." The word "sharing" might well also read "partners." In another papyri example the verb *metechō* appears alone: "as I am unable to take part in the cultivation"—as a partner in a joint enterprise.

Turning to *metochos* we find abundant evidence in the papyri where it is used as a "sharer" or "partner." Indeed, this word is translated one time in the New Testament by the word "partner." Luke 5:7 reads, "And they beckoned unto their partners [*tois metochois*], which were in the other ship, that they should come and help them." Such a usage is common in the papyri.

In two examples the feminine form (*metochē*) is used for "participation." The masculine form is found repeatedly in the sense of "partners." One such says, "Through Pasitos and the partners." One receipt reads, "We, Dionysius, son of Socrates and the associates [*metochoi*] collector of public clothing for the guards, received, etc." Another: "paid to Sotas and associates [*metochois*], collectors of money-taxes." Again: "Pikos son of Pamonthes and his colleagues to Senphaeris, greeting"— a receipt for a salt-tax. This word is also used for those who have a co-interest in a joint-enterprise, or who are joint-owners of a holding. From these it is quite clear that the word *metochos* in the papyri means "partner" or a sharer in a joint-enterprise. And this throws considerable light on its use in the New Testament.

Take, for instance, the verb *metechō*. In I Corinthians 9:10, 12 Paul compares his own situation to the Old Testament law that the ox which treads out the corn should not be muzzled (v. 9; cf. Deut. 25:4). ". . . he that thresheth in hope should be partaker [*metechein*] of his hope" (v. 10). He should share as a partner in this hope of eating some of the grain. In verse 12 he applies this truth. "If others be partakers [*metechousin*] of this power [authority] over you, are not we rather?" The least that the Corinthians can do is to make Paul a co-sharer or partner in this authority.

Earlier we noted that Moulton and Milligan cite a papyri reference in which *metechō* and *koinōneō* are used synonymously. This same usage is found in I Corinthians 10:16-17. Speaking of the Lord's Supper Paul says (v. 16) that "the cup" and "the bread" are the "communion" [*koinōnia*] of the blood and body of Christ respectively. Then in verse 17 he adds, "For we being many are one bread, and one body: for we are all partakers [*metechomen*] of that one bread." This latter verse adds immeasurably to the nature of the *koinōnia*, communion or fellowship. So closely are we related in Christ that we become joint-sharers or partners in Christ and all for which He stands (cf. Rom. 8:16-17). This involves more than merely partaking of the Lord's Supper. It includes a dedication of self and substance in the joint-enterprise of His sufferings and His glorification.

Again in I Corinthians 10:21 Paul deals with those who

continued to participate in pagan feasts but who also wanted to partake of the Lord's Supper. ". . . ye cannot be partakers of the Lord's table, and of the table of devils." Literally, "you are unable of the table of the Lord to share [*metechein*] and of the table of the devils." Note that the infinitive connects two opposites. You cannot make partners out of the Lord's table and the devil's table. Alas, how many try to do so!

The author of Hebrews shows a fondness for *metechō* and *metochos*. He uses the verb three out of the eight times it appears in the New Testament (the others in I Corinthians). With one exception (Luke 5:7, partners), he alone uses *metochos* (1:9; 3:1, 14; 6:4; 12:8).

In Hebrews 5:13 the verb is translated "useth" as one partaking of milk. In Hebrews 7:13 it is translated "pertaineth" in the sense of one belonging to the tribe of Levi. However, even here the meaning is closely related to that of co-sharing in the sense that one is a partner with others in that tribe. But the significance of this use is found in another word *heteras,* meaning another of a different kind. The author is comparing the high priesthood of Aaron and Jesus. The former is of the tribe of Levi; the latter is of the tribe of Judah. Levi was the priestly tribe. But Jesus is of a different kind of tribe which had no relationship to the priesthood. So Jesus' priesthood came by appointment from God, not as a matter of heritage.

This verse takes on added meaning when we compare it with Hebrews 2:14. Here the author speaks of Jesus sharing the nature of our flesh and blood. And here again we note the combination of *koinōneō* and *metechō* as synonymous terms. "Forasmuch then as the children are partakers [*kekoinōnēken*] of flesh and blood, he also himself took part [*meteschen*] of the same; that through death he might destroy him that had the power of death, that is, the devil." In other words as men share the nature of flesh and blood, so Jesus became their *partner* in the same. He took not the nature of angels but of the seed of Abraham (v. 16). Aaron was of a tribe separate and apart from those to whom he ministered. Jesus was identified completely, apart from sin, with those to whom he ministered. He was a co-sharer or partner in their weakness and struggles against sin. Conversely in our partnership with Him we share in His victory over sin and death, and in His power to sustain us in our continuing struggle against temptation (cf. Heb. 2:17-18).

Turning to the word *metochos* we find also the idea of partnership. In Hebrews 12:8 the author speaks of the children in a family being "partakers" (*metochoi*) in chastisement or the discipline used in training a child. This very discipline proves that we are children of our father and not "bastards." The thought is that the Christian should not chafe under such training of the Lord, for that very thing proves his sonship. We are "partners" in the family relationship as well as in the discipline. And this instruction is given that we may better fulfill our destiny as children of God.

This brings us to three most striking uses of this word. We noted in dealing with *apostasia* that the overall purpose of Hebrews is to challenge the Christian to develop and fulfill his place in God's redemptive purpose. With this thought the use of the word *metochos* agrees.

In Hebrews 3:1 the author says, "Wherefore [cf. 2:14-18, Jesus' identity with us], holy brethren, partakers [*metochoi*] of the heavenly calling, consider the Apostle and High Priest of our profession, Christ Jesus" ("Jesus" only in best manuscripts). Literally, "of the heavenly calling partners." A. T. Robertson (*Word Pictures, in loco*) refers this usage to Luke 5:7, "partners."

Now the question is as to the meaning of "heavenly calling." Definitely the call is from heaven. Is it a call to go from earth to heaven? Or is it a call from heaven to do a heavenly task? Obviously Jesus was sent (Apostle) from heaven to perform a mission for God. So the sense here would seem to be not that the Christian is a "partaker" of Christ in salvation. That thought is involved in the term "brethren." But they are "holy brethren" or brethren dedicated to the service of God. Thus it seems that *metochoi* might better be translated "partners." As Christians we are "partners" with Jesus with respect to the heavenly calling to perform God's redemptive purpose—Jesus in His death and resurrection, and we in the proclamation of the same.

This same thought is present in 3:14. We are "partners" of Christ in God's redemptive mission. As He was stedfast in His mission, so are we to be in ours. Arndt and Gingrich list this verse under the heading of "sharing or participating in" Christ, but note that "perhaps this passage belongs under" "partner, companion."

One further reference is found in Hebrews 6:4 where the author speaks of "partakers [*metochous*] of the Holy Spirit." While this could mean receiving the Holy Spirit, the New Testament teaches that even this is to the end that the Holy Spirit might not only seal us unto the day of final redemption, but also might work through us in carrying out God's redemptive purpose. So even here we are "partners of the Holy Spirit" to that end.

It is quite clear, then, that the word *metochos* and its related terms refer not merely to a privilege which the Christian receives, but more definitely to a responsibility to be discharged.

OLIGOS

(An Interrupted Sermon)

This adjective is found often in both the papyri and in the New Testament (43 times). Its basic meaning is "few," "little," or "small."

Examples of this word occur frequently in the papyri. It is used with respect to time, number, and degree. One instance of time reads, "Play the man, for a little (*oligos*) time is to you. . . ." When used with the negative particle it means the opposite of "few" or "little"— e.g., *ouk oligēn elan,* "a quantity [many] of olives" (number); "whereby I have suffered no slight (*ouk oligou*) damage" (degree). One instance renders it as "short-sighted" (*oligon blepōn*).

Certain instances use the word preceded by a preposition which in each case colors the meaning of the word. One such is *di' oligōn*, "briefly" (cf. I Peter 5:12) found in an example dated in the second century B.C. "In a few words [*di' oliōn*, *oligos* written without the *gamma* or "g"] to set before you. . . ." *Meta* (after) is combined with this word to read "after a little." With the preposition *pros* (for) it means "for a short time" (cf. I Tim. 4:8a; James 4:14).

Of special interest is the use of this word with the preposition *en*. In Ephesians 3:3 *en oligōi* reads "in a few words" (AV). The marginal reading is "a little before." But A. T. Robertson rules this out, noting that had Paul meant this he would have used *pro oligou*, "shortly before." This usage in Ephesians sheds light on Acts 26:28-29 which is given various renderings by various scholars.

"Then Agrippa said unto Paul, Almost thou persuadest me to be a Christian" (AV). This reading is rejected by most modern authorities. Instead it is variously translated "briefly" (Williams), "in a little while," "with a little effort." A. T. Robertson renders it "with a little persuasion. . . ."

Arndt and Gingrich cite Aristotle's use of this phrase for "in brief," relating it to Ephesians 3:3. Furthermore, they cite Pindar and Plato for the meaning "in a short time, quickly," relating these meanings to Acts 26:28. At any rate the phrase *en oligōi* may well mean "in a little time," "in a few words," or "in a little effort." It might also mean "in short" or "in a summation" of the matter. Certainly it does not mean "almost," for to say this Agrippa would have used *oligou, par' oligon,* or *dei liogou* (Robertson).

Agrippa evidently was not under conviction as the Authorized Version would indicate. He was a profligate Jew who at this very moment was living with His sister as man and wife. He was more of a Roman than a Jew in interest. So when Paul assumed that he believed the prophets (Acts 26:27), Agrippa interrupted him. He was not interested in religion.

So, having heard enough, he merely ended the interview or sermon. In effect, with a shrug of his shoulders, he said, "In short you are persuading me to make me a Christian." This effect is evident whether one follows this meaning "in a short time," "quickly," or "with but little effort." Alas, how many people cut the preacher short by tuning his message out of their minds and hearts!

Verse 29 presents some difficulty for this rendering. For Paul replied that he wished that "in little and in much" (*en oligōi kai en megalōi*) both Agrippa and the others hearing him might become as he was, except for his bonds. Some scholars hold that for *en oligōi* to mean "in a little time" Paul should have used *en pollōi,* which reading is found in some manuscripts. But *en megalōi* is most probably genuine. However, Arndt and Gingrich render this phrase "whether in a short time or in a long time." Paul makes a play on Agrippa's words as with respect he answers the king's curt interruption.

But this sermon was ended abruptly nevertheless as Agrippa, Festus, and Bernice rose up, went aside, and conferred not on the spiritual but on the political aspects of the matter. They had the opportunity to hear "the greatest story ever told," but refused it with sarcasm.

PAIDAGŌGOS

(A Boy-Leader)

This term literally means a "boy-leader." From it comes the word "pedagogue." Variously the word may be rendered "tutor," "attendant," "custodian," or "guide." Among the Greeks and Romans it was applied to a trusted slave whose duty it was to supervise the life and morals of a boy until he reached maturity, or from about six to sixteen. Until this latter age a boy was not even allowed to leave the house except in the company of his *paidagōgos*. He was the boy's tutor until such time that he was ready to be taught by a regular teacher (*didaskalos*). The *paidagōgos* was not a teacher in the usual sense of that word. When the child was old enough to go to a teacher, the *paidagōgos* conducted him to and from school. After he reached maturity he no longer needed the care of such a person.

Moulton and Milligan list one papyri example of this word which illustrates the dual nature of tutor and leader to the teacher. A mother writes to her son with respect to his education as follows: "Let it be the care of both you and your attendant [*paidagōgos*] that you go to a suitable teacher." She concludes, "Salute your highly esteemed attendant Eros." In this case the "attendant" bore the responsibility with the boy of choosing the teacher. The admonition to esteem the attendant implies respect for him as a "tutor."

There are only three uses of this word in the New Testament (I Cor. 4:15; Gal. 3:24-25). In I Corinthians 4:15 Paul likens Apollos and the others to "tutors," whereas he is the spiritual father of the Corinthian Christians. Paul founded the church there. The others are tutors to watch over them on behalf of the *father*. They should respect their tutors, but not allow them to take the place of their *father*. Implied also is the sterner discipline of Paul as *father* over that of the tutors.

The most striking example of this word is seen in Galatians 3:24-25. Here the law is the *paidagōgos*. The Galatians had been tutored by the law with respect to moral principles. But it was not their final teacher. Its basic function was to conduct them to Christ, the true Teacher. This it did by arousing their consciousness of sin. But since it could not remove the power of sin, it led them to Him who could do so. This coming to Christ Paul likens to their faith by which they were justified.

But from the papyri example we learn that while the *paidagōgos* might choose "a suitable teacher," the child also must concur in the choice. The "law" points to Christ. But

38239

we must concur in this choice if He is to become our Teacher. A child who chooses rather to remain with the *paidagōgos* will miss the maturity and freedom which the Teacher offers. The "law" is not to be disregarded as of no moral value. As the boy was to esteem his *paidagōgos,* so are we to esteem the moral and spiritual values contained in the law. But we are not merely to remain under it. Instead we are to follow its office as "tutor" as it points or leads us to Christ, the Teacher.

In verse 25 "faith" is seen as the state of maturity. Having reached this goal, they no longer need the *paidagōgos.* The *paidagōgos* speaks of the confinement which was under the law. Under the Teacher they are made free or mature.

The figure of the *paidagōgos* and the Teacher enhances the meaning of Matthew 11:29. "Take my yoke upon you, and learn of me. . . ." To take the yoke was a rabbinical figure for enrolling as a pupil under a teacher. Coming to Christ one is freed from the restricting yoke of the *paidagōgos* to wear the yoke of Christ which does not rub nor does it weigh one down to the burden of sin which the law could not remove.

Are you still under the *paidagōgos,* or have you allowed him to bring you to Christ?

PANĒGURIS

(O Happy Day!)

This word appears only one time in the New Testament, but this one use is most meaningful. It is translated "general assembly" (Heb. 12:23). In the Septuagint it is found in Ezekiel 46:11; Hosea 3:11, 13; 9:5; and Amos 5:21. The basic meaning of the word is "festival" or "festal gathering."

The meaning is amply borne out in the papyri. One instance uses it simply of a public gathering. But the festal idea is clearly shown in such usages as "with the exception of markets and festivals" (literally, "apart from markets with festivals"); and "tradition, no less than the distinguished character of the festival, requires that the *ephebi* should do their utmost in the gymnastic display." Another example suggests an invitation to a birthday party: "deign to gladden the birthday festival of my son Gennadius." In the inscriptions this word is used of both religious and social occasions. It appears often in classical Greek as "festival." Moulton and Milligan cite other examples, suggesting that in Hebrews 12:23 the word should be translated "festal assembly."

Scholars are divided as to the reference contained in the word as used in Hebrews 12:23. Since the language and punctuation are not clear, several possibilities exist. One thing is certain. The author contrasts the awesome and fearful atmosphere of Mt. Sinai (12:18-21) with the festive atmosphere of Mt. Zion or heaven. The former suggests the giving of the law and the subsequent covenant with Israel. The latter speaks of grace and the new covenant in Christ.

Turning to the meaning of *panēguris* Marcus Dods (*Expositor's Greek Testament*) suggests three possible connotations. (1) "General assembly [*panēguris*] and church of the first-born" may be in apposition with "an innumerable company [myriads] of angels." Thus it would mean a festive gathering in heaven composed of angels and the glorified saints in heaven. (2) A new particular or group may be introduced with the words "and to the church of the firstborn" as separate from "angels." (3) A new particular may be seen in "to myriads of angels, to a festal gathering and assembly of the firstborn." Dods favors the first possibility.

However, there is much to be said for the second and/or third or a combination of both. If we examine the remainder of the passage several things seem likely which would separate the "angels" from "the church of the firstborn." Their names are "written in heaven" (Heb. 12:23; cf. Luke 10:20; Phil. 3:20, "conversation" is "colony," Moffatt; 4:3; Rev. 13:8; 20:11-15). They are to appear before God for judgment (Heb. 12:23). They are there through the blood of the new covenant

(Heb. 12:24). None of these applies to angels, which, of course, no one holds.

But this does seem significant when we endeavor to determine whether or not *panēguris* is to be related to "myriads of angels" or to "the church of the firstborn." In the Greek text this word joins the two phrases. But to which does it refer? It is of interest to note that one manuscript ("D") reads "myriads of saints, a festal assembly, and the church of the firstborn." But this most likely is not a true reading.

Westcott raises an interesting question. Should "angels" be related to "myriads" or to "festal assembly"? He says that the rhythm of the sentence naturally relates it to "myriads." If so, then he notes that *panēguris* standing alone is a "harsh" construction. But is not this exactly what the author intended?

If so, this word carries with it the idea of an *exclamation,* an announcement, the blast of a trumpet calling the people to the festal assembly, and the joyful shouts of those who rejoice and sing (cf. Rev. 19:1, 4-7). Let us note also in this passage the conjunction "and" (*kai*). But this word may also be translated "even." If this be followed, the entire passage may well read, "But ye are come to mount Zion, even to the city of the living God, to the heavenly Jerusalem, and to myriads of angels; to a festal assembly! even to the church of the firstborn, the ones having been written in heaven, and to God the Judge of all, and to the spirits of the justified ones having been made perfect, and to Jesus the mediator of a new covenant, and to the blood of sprinkling. . ." (Heb. 12:22-24).

However one relates *panēguris* the thought is that of a festal assembly in heaven when all of the true church shall be gathered in the presence of God. This is in contrast with the assembly of Israel before God at Sinai which was characterized by fear and quaking (v. 21). But before "mount Zion" (v. 22) there will be joy and gladness. No matter about the judgment before the God of all! For in our Mediator of the new covenant we will have been judged, justified, and made perfect. It will be a "festal assembly" indeed as we sit at the marriage feast of the Lamb (cf. Rev. 19:6-9), and as "a bride adorned [in God's righteousness] for her husband" (Rev. 21:2-4) we go out "to meet the bridegroom" (Matt. 25:1ff.). It will be a "festal assembly" indeed!

A "festal assembly! even to the church of the firstborn having been enrolled in heaven!"

PARATITHĒMI

(Placed on Deposit)

This verb is a combination of *tithēmi*, I place, and *para*, alongside. Literally it means "I place alongside." It is also used in the sense of "set before" as of food. This verb form appears nineteen times in the New Testament (cf. Mark 6:41; I Tim. 1:18; I Peter 4:19). The noun *parathēkē* is used three times (I Tim. 6:20; II Tim. 1:12, 14). Both words are used repeatedly in the papyri.

The verb form (*paratithēmi*) is used literally of setting an "ink pot" beside or before one. It is found in an account where "the veteran straightway ran and reported [*parētheto*] it to his lord." Also it is found as *"evidence . . .* concerning parentage" (author's italics). Furthermore, a derivative of this word (*paretethē*) is found as the heading for a registration of a claim to ownership meaning "inserted in the register." In the middle voice it is employed in the sense of depositing with another that which is one's own, as depositing money in a bank. It also connotes to "commend" a person to the care of another as in a letter of recommendation.

The noun form (*parathēkē*) is likewise used in the sense of "deposit": "I have received from Aphrodisius 1500 drachmae as *deposit*" (author's italics); "I declare to have from you in deposit 300 drachmae to be paid back in May-June."

When these various meanings are applied to the New Testament usage many thoughts appear. The obvious meaning is present in various references of setting food before one (Mark 8:6-7; I Cor. 10:27). In more picturesque fashion Paul places on deposit (middle voice) with Timothy the charge to be a good soldier of Christ (I Tim. 1:18). In turn Timothy is to place on deposit with faithful men the things which he has heard from Paul (II Tim. 2:2). Both are to be guarded and used for their intended purposes.

Worthy of note is the fact that some manuscripts of I Timothy 6:20 and II Timothy 1:14 use *parakatathēkē*. This is a stronger form of the noun. It is found in the papyri of "a secure deposit, subject to no claim or charge." Both Moulton and Milligan and Arndt and Gingrich cite these references for this word. The latter notes that this is the real Attic form, but that the two words may be used interchangeably.

Elders were ordained and placed on deposit with the Lord for safe keeping and use (Acts 14:23; cf. 20:32). The souls of Christian martyrs are placed on deposit with God for safe keeping (I Peter 4:19). And Paul is persuaded that Christ is able to guard that which he has placed on deposit with Him for safekeeping and to deliver it to him in the resurrection (II Tim. 1:12). Arndt and Gingrich note that both *parathēkē and parakatathēkē* are used with the word "to guard," suggesting safe keeping.

However, the mother lode of this word in the New Testament is found in Jesus' last word from the cross. "Father, into thy hands I commend my spirit" (Luke 23:46). The word "commend" renders the word *paratithemai* (middle voice). This very word is used in the papyri of commending one into the care of another, e.g., a letter of recommendation. Thus as Paul committed his soul to Christ for safekeeping until the resurrection (II Tim. 1:12), so Jesus commits His soul to the Father until His resurrection. Did He not also recommend Himself, on the basis of His death, as the Saviour of the world?

Carrying the thought in this word further, Jesus in His spirit set before the Father the evidence of the atonement for sin (cf. Heb. 9:12, 24). He "reported" to the Father His successful completion of a mission. He declared the "evidence," not of parentage, but of His complete identity with lost men as their Saviour. He "inserted" into the registry of heaven His claim to ownership of all who would believe on Him. In these words Jesus took His atoning work and placed it on deposit with the Father to be guarded and used for the purpose for which it is intended. He placed Himself alongside the Father, "from henceforth expecting till his enemies be made his footstool" (Heb. 10:13).

Because Jesus *commended* His spirit to the Father, in confidence men may place on deposit their souls with Him, knowing that they are guarded and safe against the final day of resurrection and judgment.

PAROUSIA

(The Visit of the King!)

This word comes from a compound Greek verb *para*, alongside, near, or at, and *eimi*, the word for essential being. Thus the noun form basically means "presence." It is so used in classic Greek and other contemporary writings.

In the papyri this meaning is found in several examples: "the repair of what has been swept away by the river requires my presence" [*parousias*]; a man writes to his brothers, "We await your presence;" "it is no use if a person comes too late for what required his presence;" a man swore in the "presence of the bishops and of his own brothers."

In this sense the word is used in the New Testament. Paul's enemies in Corinth said that his letters were "weighty and powerful; but his bodily presence is weak. . ." (II Cor. 10:10). In Philippians 2:12 he speaks of his "presence" and his "absence." In this same sense Paul uses *parousia* for "coming" (I Cor. 16:17; II Cor. 7:6-7; Phil. 1:26).

However, for students of the New Testament its most vital meaning has to do with the "visit" of a king, emperor, or some other person of authority. The word *parousia* was used as a technical term to express this idea. Usually taxes were imposed to prepare for such an event. For instance, one papyri example speaks of contributions to make a "crown" to be presented to the king on his "arrival" (*parousias*). A certain Appenneus writes that he has prepared a number of birds for consumption at "the visit of Chrysippus," a ruler. Mention is made of a tax of "80 arbatae of wheat for the supplies imposed in connexion with the king's visit." And one such example appears where certain ones laid their grievances before King Ptolemy Philometor and Queen Cleopatra on the occasion of their royal visits to Memphis.

Such uses throw great light on certain passages in the New Testament.

For instance, this word *parousia* is used of the "coming" of "that Wicked" (antichrist) (II Thess. 2:9). It is used of the "coming of the day of God. . ." (II Peter 3:12).

Repeatedly this word is found with reference to the second "coming" of Christ (Matt. 24:3, 27, 37, 39; I Cor. 15:23; I Thess. 2:19; 3:13; 4:15; 5:23; II Thess. 2:1; James 5:7, 8; II Peter 1:16; 3:4; I John 2:28). Thus the return of the Lord is likened to the visit of a king or emperor to his people.

Relating this thought to the papyri examples several meanings appear. The Lord's return will be *official* (Matt. 24:30). His subjects must at great sacrifice prepare for His coming (Matt. 24:45ff.). When He comes He must be *crowned* Lord of all (Rev. 4:10f.). It will be a festive occasion for those who prepare for Him (Matt. 25:1ff.). When He appears judgment will ensue, when all wrongs will be righted, and the evil-doers punished (Matt. 25:19ff.). Patience should characterize those who await His coming (James 5:7-8; II Peter 3:4). Despite His long-awaited coming, it will be sudden. Woe betide him who fails to be ready (Matt. 24:44ff.). The subjects of the

Lord should pray that their King shall hasten His *parousia* (Rev. 22:20).

This is the glorious and blessed hope of every Christian (Titus 2:13). Deissmann related this word to Zechariah 9:9, "Rejoice greatly, O daughter of Zion; shout, O daughter of Jerusalem: behold, thy King cometh unto thee: he is just, and having salvation; lowly, and riding upon an ass, and upon a colt the foal of an ass" (cf. Matt. 21:5).

"Even so, come, Lord Jesus" (Rev. 22:20).

PHATNĒ

(Jesus' Birth Place)

Where was Jesus born, in a stable, cave, or under the open sky? The answer depends upon how one regards this word. For the meaning of the word itself is inconclusive.

Phatnē comes from the verb *pateomai,* to eat. So the word is traditionally translated "manger" (Luke 2:7, 12, 16) or "stall" (Luke 13:15). But its literal meaning is "feeding place" or "feeding trough." Where was this feeding trough? Tradition (Justin Martyr) places it in a cave or some place connected with the inn. But is tradition correct? What does the papyri say?

Moulton and Milligan list two examples. One simply reads "to one feeding trough" (*heni phatnēi*). The other "to a feeding trough" (*phatnas*). But here it is used with the derivative of a word referring to feeding as with grass (*chortazō*). Two noun forms of this verb are *chortos* (an inclosure or pasture-ground) and *chortasma* (pasture or provender for cattle). From this connection H. J. Cadbury concludes that "this much at least is probable, that *phatnē* is a place in the open and that the clause which follows emphasizes the absence of shelter." Arndt and Gingrich comment that the word "could perhaps be the *stable* . . . or even a *feeding-place* under the open sky, in contrast to *kataluma* [inn], the shelter where people stayed."

Either meaning could apply in Luke 13:15 where *phatnē* is translated "stall." However, it just as well could mean that the owner of the animal untied it from the feeding trough and led it away to drink wherever either might be.

But a further consideration may help. At what time of year was Jesus born? Scholars generally agree that it was not in December, since the shepherds had their flocks in the open fields. The enrollment for taxes would more likely have been set at a time of year more suitable for travel, perhaps between the early and late harvests, or between the last of June and the first of October. Sometime in August is more likely. This would allow for travel to and from the place of enrollment between the two harvests.

The strong pull of tradition leads some authorities to surmise that the animals were in the field, hence the empty stable. But it is just as true to the text to say that the "feeding trough" was also in the fields of Bethlehem near to the animals, or else out in the open in Bethlehem itself. Reference to the Magi entering "the house" (Matt. 2:11) does not enter into the decision. Their visit was at least six weeks, some say two years, after Jesus' birth. The fact that the shepherds came to Bethlehem does not speak conclusively either way (Luke 2:15).

To be sure one cannot be dogmatic, since *phatnē* has no reference to the place. But in view of the probable season of Jesus' birth, plus the evidence in the papyri, it is possible that Jesus was born in Bethlehem but under the open sky. If so, truly

> "The stars in the sky looked down where He lay,
> The little Lord Jesus asleep in the hay."

stood as "confidence" or "commitment" on the basis of the truth of the gospel. In Titus 2:10 the thought is that a Christian slave should so live as to be the very embodiment of that which is worthy of confidence. Hebrews 10:39 may be rendered "but of confidence with respect to the saving of the soul."

A most interesting use of *pistis* is seen in Romans 3:26 where it is translated as though it were a verb. ". . . of him which believeth in Jesus" reads literally, "the out of faith of Jesus." "Out of " is *ek* or the source of a thing. So the source is "faith of Jesus." Does this refer to Jesus' faithfulness in performing God's act of justification? It could. Or it could mean the *faith* of man by which he is relying upon Jesus' redemptive act for his salvation. But in either case the thought of *confidence* or *reliability* is present. *Expositor's* says, "*Ton ek pisteōs Jesou* is every one who is properly and sufficiently characterized as a believer in Jesus" or who has committed himself to Jesus in confidence.

Pistos is found in the papyri in the sense of "faithful" or "trustworthy." Three examples will suffice: "I have handed her over [note commitment] to the good and faithful men among the grave-diggers themselves that they may take care of her"; "true and trustworthy advocates"; a slave is described as "faithful [worthy of trust] and not given to running away." In rare instances the word is used in the sense of one who is "trusting" or "believing."

These serve to show the meaning in fifty-three out of sixty-six usages in the New Testament where it is translated "faithful" (cf. Matt. 24:45; 25:21-23; Acts 16:15; I Cor. 1:9). In each instance, the thought of trustworthiness is present.

In the rare sense of "trusting" or "believing" this word is found eight times (John 20:27; Acts 10:45; 16:1; II Cor. 6:15; I Tim. 4:3, 10; 5:16; 6:2). In each case the thought is that of one who has committed himself to Christ (cf. I Tim. 4:12). In II Corinthians 1:18 (cf. I Cor. 1:9) and I Timothy 3:1 "true" may be rendered "faithful" or "trustworthy" (cf. III John 5). Acts 13:34 may be read "the trustworthy mercies of David."

It is clear, therefore, that the basic thought in *pisteuō* and its derivatives is that of committing oneself to someone or something with the confidence that the commitment is safe and sure. "Commitment" also involves one's service for Christ. This is the true essence of faith.

SKĒNOŌ

(Dwelling in a Tent)

This word denotes the idea of living or dwelling as in a tent. Since tents were used as dwelling places, the thought may be that of temporary or settled dwelling. When used of heaven, in the very nature of the case the word carries the idea of permanency. But when it connotes an earthly tent or tabernacle the thought is that of something which may be taken down quickly and moved to another location. The noun forms *skēnē* and *skēnos* refer to a tent or a tabernacle which was made of either green branches, skins, or other woven material. Paul was a tentmaker (*skēnopoios*, Acts 18:3).

In the secular papyri we would expect *skēnoō* to denote temporary dwelling. And while the New Testament usages carry the idea of dwelling in tents (after the fashion of the ancient Israelites), in the papyri the sense is more that of temporary dwelling in a house. One example dated in the third century B.C. reads "dwelling [*skēnōn*] in the house of Aristobulus." The idea of temporary dwelling in a house is clearly seen in another example of the same period: "dwelling in the house" (*oikia*). Apparently these refer to *visits*, not permanent dwelling.

In the papyri *skēnē* is spoken of as "a tent made of skin" or leather (cf. Matt. 3:4; Mark 1:6 of John's girdle). Another example reads, "But you may not come out of your tent." Two uses of the word refer to a ship's "cabin." Moulton and

Milligan note that skēnē used for *oikia* (house) is of Asiatic origin, because of the Asiatic custom of dwelling in tents.

The word *skēnos* does not appear in the papyri. But an inscription over a tomb employs it in the sense of the body being the "tent" of the soul.

A study of these words in the New Testament is most revealing. For instance, *skēnoō* is used in John 1:14. "And the Word was made flesh [came into being as flesh], and dwelt among [*en*, in the sphere of] us. . . ." This speaks of the temporary incarnation of God as of Christ dwelling in a tent.

This verb appears four times in Revelation with various meanings. In 7:15 it speaks of God who "shall dwell among them" (redeemed saints in heaven). But here *skēnoō* is followed by the preposition *epi*, over or above. So the sense is that God will pitch His tent of protection *over* them. In 12:12 and 13:6 the figure is that of the saints dwelling in heaven, a permanent dwelling; but this is in keeping with certain papyri usages. In 21:3 we find both the noun (*skēnē*, tent or tabernacle, cf. 13:6) and the verb. Here the sense of *skēnē* is that of God's "tabernacle" in which God *dwells*. This is the heavenly, permanent tabernacle in contrast to the earthly, temporary tabernacle in the wilderness. In the wilderness and beyond God dwelt in the tabernacle as a symbol of His presence with His people. But He was accessible only through the high priest. Here God dwells "with them" or *among* them. This intimate *Presence* is emphasized in "God himself shall be among them."

An interesting example of this verb is found in II Corinthians 12:9. Here it has the prefix *epi* (*episkēnoō*). It means to dwell *over* or *upon*. The meaning could be that the "power of Christ" might dwell *over* Paul in the sense of protection (cf. Rev. 7:15). Or it could mean that the "power of Christ" might dwell upon him to empower him for service. Either makes sense, but the latter seems more likely here. But the use of *skēnoō* (with *epi*) also suggests the possibility of Christ's power being removed if Paul glories in his own strength rather than that of God (cf. II Cor. 12:9, "my strength is made perfect in [thy] weakness"). This is a thought for every Christian to ponder.

Turning to *skēnē* other interesting ideas appear. In Matthew 17:4 it is used in the sense of "booths" made of green branches (cf. Mark 9:5; Luke 9:33). This was just before the Feast of Tabernacles which involved sitting under such booths.

In Acts 7:43-44 a contrast is drawn between pagan and Hebrew worship as seen in the "tabernacle of Moloch" and that of God. In Hebrews 8:2, 9 the contrast is between the heavenly and earthly tabernacles of God. In Hebrews 9:2-3 this word is used of the two divisions of the Hebrew tabernacle (cf. vv. 6-7, 21). But 9:11 speaks of the heavenly tabernacle. In Hebrews 9:8-10 the reference is to the ceremonies involved in the Hebrew tabernacle. Here the word may also be understood for the *temple* in Jerusalem which was still standing but soon to pass away.

In Hebrews 11:9 the word "tabernacles" should read "tents." It speaks of Abraham's temporary sojourn on earth as he looked for the city of God or heaven. A tent fastened to the ground by pegs was temporary. A "city which hath foundations" was permanent.

In Revelation 13:6 the "tabernacle" speaks not only of a place of worship but of all that pertains to God. And in 15:5 "the temple of the tabernacle" reads "the Holy of Holies [*naos*] of the tabernacle." The *naos* was behind the veil in the earthly tabernacle where God dwelt in mercy. But in the heavenly tabernacle this *naos* is opened, and from it [*ek tou naou*] came seven angels bearing seven plagues. So the God of mercy is also the God of judgment. The thought of the permanency of the heavenly tabernacle in Revelation 21:3 is anticipated by Jesus when He said, ". . .they may receive you into everlasting habitations" (*skēnas,* dwelling places, Luke 16:9).

In Acts 15:16 the "tabernacle of David" refers to all those who are redeemed by Christ. When the exiles returned from Babylon they rebuilt the temple of Solomon or a temple to replace it. The reference in Amos 9:11-12 did refer to the restoration of the temple in Jerusalem and its ministry. But Peter sees its greater meaning as being fulfilled in the redemptive work of the Son of David, whereby truly both Israel and the "heathen" (Amos 9:12; "Gentiles," Acts 15:17) may be built into the "tabernacle of David."

The word *skēnos* is found in the New Testament only in II Corinthians 5:1, 4. Here Paul uses it to refer to the temporary abiding place ("earthly house") of the spirit, and which is to be replaced by a "building of God, an house not made with hands, eternal in the heavens" (cf. Heb. 11:9f.; II Peter 1:13f., *skēnōma*). "Were dissolved" is the very word used for striking down a tent. So Paul looks forward to moving out of a tent and into a house built by God (cf. II Cor. 5:1-8).

What a wonderful hope for the believer! A tent struck down and a house built of God. ". . .absent from the body. . . present with the Lord. . . ."

SKLĒROS

(Hard as Rock)

The verb form of this word is *sklērunō* meaning "to harden." One example is found in the papyri. It was also used by Galen and Hippocrates in the medical sense. This usage of the word survives in modern medical language in such words as "scleroderma," hardness of the skin; "scleroma," a hard tumor; and "sclerosis," the hardening of body tissues.

The noun *sklērotēs* is found one time in the papyri and once in Romans 2:5 as "hardness" of heart. It may well be rendered "obstinacy" or "stubbornness." Or it may be rendered "stubbornness of will."

Sklēros is the adjective form meaning "hard" or "rough"

as to the touch. In one papyri example it is used in this dual sense as of "hard" stone (also in the inscriptions). One citation renders it as "bitter (or pickled) meats," which adds flavor to the meaning with regard to attitude. In one case it is used metaphorically: "This did not seem to be hard" or "harsh." A similar usage is found in an inscription (Kaibel) where kings are described as "both inhuman and harsh." This also sheds light on certain usages in the New Testament. The word *sklērourgos* is found for "stone-mason." In one instance *sklēros* is combined with *trachēlos,* "neck," *sklērotrachēlos,* meaning "stiff-neck." One such example is found in Acts 7:51. Note also *sklērokardia,* "hard-hearted" (not found in papyri, but cf. Matt. 19:8; Mark 10:5). These carry a certain medical flavor, but are metaphors for unyielding wills and lack of spiritual sensitivity and understanding respectively.

These same ideas are present in the use of *sklērunō* in Acts 19:9 and Hebrews 3:8, 13, 15; 4:7. The example in Romans 9:18 is the source of theological difficulty. Did God arbitrarily harden Pharaoh's heart? If so, was Pharaoh responsible? Exodus 8:15, 32; 9:4 say that Pharaoh hardened his own heart. Of course, the subject under discussion in Romans is the sovereignty of God, whereby God acts within His own will but in keeping with His nature and purpose. The point in this passage is that Pharaoh repeatedly hardened his heart in the face of God's wonderful works. God will not violate a human personality or will. Thus God simply acted in accord with His nature and purpose by recognizing the hardness which existed in Pharaoh's heart. The present tense of the verb in Romans 9:18 would seem to allow this. Thus Pharaoh's heart was hardened, not by God's perpetration but by His permission.

The medical sense of this word by Galen and Hippocrates sheds light on this passage. The doctor does not cause the hardening. But he acts in the light of the fact of it. As God acts in accord with His nature and purpose, He did not cause Pharaoh's stubbornness. But since He wills not to violate one's personality, He accepted the fact of Pharaoh's condition.

And since God's holiness is in unyielding opposition to evil, He acted accordingly.

The adjective *sklēros* appears five times in the New Testament (not in best mss. in Acts 9:5). And in all instances save one it is rendered as "hard." Acts 26:14 reads, "It is hard for thee to kick against the pricks." Here "hard" is used in the metaphorical sense. A "prick" was a pointed stick used to goad an ox. Page notes that it is taken from the figure of an ox which kicks against the prick, and which receives a severer wound. In Paul's case the "prick" was the call of God stemming from Saul's experience in seeing the manner in which Stephen died. Stephen saw the Lord Jesus alive (Acts 7:55-56). And now Saul sees or hears Him. Thus he receives the severer wound in his soul because of his attitude toward Jesus. It was indeed "hard."

John 6:60 reads, "This is an hard [harsh] saying; who can hear it?" The "saying" was Jesus' words about eating His flesh and drinking His blood. Failing to rise to the significance of this symbolism, the multitude thought of cannibalism or pagan worship. Thus it was "harsh" to their ears. The hardness was not in the "saying" but in their hearts.

In James 3:4 the word is translated "fierce." This is with reference to wind (nature). Howson notes that James in one short epistle draws more imagery from natural phenomena than is found in all of Paul's writings. The picture is that of a strong, stiff, harsh, hard, rough wind. A. T. Robertson renders it "rough," which is in keeping with the papyri usage of something that is rough to the touch.

Jude 15 uses the word "hard" with respect to that which "ungodly sinners have spoken against him" (Lord). The word here might better be rendered "harsh" as *harsh speakers*.

Much light is thrown on Matthew 25:24 by Kaibel's *inscription*, not papyri, cited above in the example of kings being called "both inhuman and harsh." While the word "inhuman" (*anēmeroi*) does not appear in Matthew 25:24 the thought is implied. So the unfaithful servant may be understood as saying that his owner was an "inhuman and harsh man."

TELEŌ, TELEIOŌ

(The Means to an End)

These two words, while distinct as to meaning, are closely related both in the papyri and in the New Testament. Basically the former means to finish or to bring to a desired end. The latter speaks of that desired end or to make perfect. The latter deals primarily with the goal in view; the former deals with the act of achieving that goal. But at times their meaning seems to be interchangeable. However, the fine distinction between the two words may be seen in John 19:28. "After this, Jesus knowing that all things were now accomplished [teleō, brought to a desired end], that the scriptures might be fulfilled [teleioō, made perfect or complete, the end desired] . . . ."

The papyri is fraught with examples of both words and their related terms. For instance, teleiōsis, from teleioō, is used in the following: "I have dispatched as my agent Heraclides. . .to *conclude* the transaction" (author's italics). Another example employs teleō in the sense of "accomplish": "until you accomplish this for me." The former speaks of that which is to be done. The latter speaks of the doing of it.

One of the most enlightening uses of teleioō in the papyri has to do with "execute" as of a deed in the proper way. One such use is that of completing a deed by the insertion of the date and signatures. By inference teleō would refer to the act of doing so.

Teleō itself is used in the sense of paying taxes or rent—that which is due another for the privilege (cf. teleios) of living in a country or in a house. It is also used of a promissory note: "I will pay you this sum." Furthermore, receipts are often introduced by the phrase tetelestai. This is the very word used by Jesus on the cross, "It is finished" (John 19:30).

Applying these various ideas to the New Testament usage of these words and their derivatives yields much fruit. For example, note the distinction between the words *teleioō* and *teleō* respectively as the desired goal and the means to that goal. The verb *teleioō* appears in Hebrews nine of the twenty-four times used in the New Testament (2:10; 5:9; 7:19, 28; 9:9; 10:1, 14; 11:40; 12:23). In each instance it speaks of a condition to be obtained. The verb *teleō*, the means to the end, does not appear in Hebrews, but the thought is everywhere present. For instance, in 2:10 "perfect" is the goal, "sufferings" is the means. This thought is seen also in 5:9; 7:19; 10:14; 12:23. In 7:28 the consecration is an act of God. In 9:9; 10:1 the goal is stated but the means is lacking. In 11:40 the goal is envisioned, the means of which is the faithfulness of subsequent generations of Christians in fulfilling their part in the redemptive purpose of God.

But the richest use of these related words is found in John 19:28, 30. Note above the relation of these two words in 19:28. In 19:30 Jesus cried, "It is finished" (*tetelestai*). This is a perfect indicative passive form of the verb *teleō*. The perfect tense speaks of a finished and permanent work. The indicative mode connotes its certainty. The passive voice means that this is something done for one by another. That which is to be accomplished is the condition (*teleioō*, cf. 19:28) whereby man may have a right relation with God. This has been accomplished by Jesus' suffering and death on the cross. Thus just before Jesus dismissed His spirit He cried, "That which is required is finished."

Therefore, Jesus cries to the Father, "I have finished the mission which you sent me to accomplish." "The deed is dated and signed in my blood." The tax or rent (ransom) which the Father demanded has been paid. Man can now live in the Father's kingdom or family. In eternity the Son signed a promissory note for man's redemption. It is now paid. The receipt for this payment is introduced with the word "*tetelestai*."

One can well imagine that host of Old Testament saints,

saved on credit or by a promissory note, in heaven but with their deeds not yet dated and signed. What glorious news was this shout of victory from the cross! Indeed, what "good news" it is to all men who will hear, heed, and believe this glorious gospel!

It should be remembered, however, that *teleioō* refers to a deed completed by adding the date and *signatures* (plural). Jesus dated and signed the deed. Have you?

XENOS, PAREPIDĒMOS, PAROIKOS

(Strangers in a Strange Land)

The writer will never forget the feeling which crept over him when, on a boat train to Paris, someone said, "Do you realize that we are all foreigners?" That is the thought contained in the word *xenos*. For a *xenos* was a foreigner or alien in contrast to a citizen (*politēs*). A *xenos* was one who was just passing through a land. When used as an adjective it meant "strange," "foreign," or "unfamiliar."

That "foreigners" had a rough time in the ancient world is borne out in the papyri. One man writes that he was despised by everyone "because I am a stranger" (*xenos*). Another writes home to his family, "Do not be anxious about me because I am away from home, for I am personally acquainted with these places and am not a stranger here." In a Christian letter of the fourth century A.D. one writes, "It is better for you to be in your own homes whatever they may be, than abroad" or in a strange or foreign land (*epi xenēs*). In an account of a dining club those present were distinguished as "members" (*sundeipnoi*, members or dinner-partners) and "guests" (*xenoi*). The "guests" were there as a privilege rather than a right. This throws light on III John 5.

Two words related in meaning to *xenos* are *parepidēmos* and *paroikos*. The former refers to a foreigner who is a "sojourner," a "pilgrim" or one taking up temporary residence in an alien land but not becoming a part of its life. This thought is present in several papyri examples, and is carried over into the New Testament (cf. Heb. 11:13; I Peter 1:1; 2:11). One inscription combines *parepidēmos* and *xenos*, "of the sojourn [or pilgrimage] of foreigners."

Paroikos means a foreigner who is a "licensed sojourner." This person became a *resident alien* by the payment of a small tax. Thus he was privileged to live in a country and enter into its life short of citizenship, usually business, although he kept his citizenship in another country. This word is found in both the papyri and inscriptions. It is found in the New Testament in Acts 7:6, 29; Ephesians 2:19; I Peter 2:11. The verb form (*paroikeō*) is used in Luke 24:18 and Hebrews 11:9. See also *paroikia* in Acts 13:7 and I Peter 1:17.

Xenos appears fourteen times in the New Testament. In Matthew 25:35, 38, 43, 44 it speaks of "foreigners" who were welcomed or not welcomed. The presence or lack of a Christian attitude is shown in one's treatment of a *xenos*. In the light of the harsh treatment usually given to them, the contrast between the conduct of the Christian and the non-Christian is sharply drawn. This is a timely lesson for our day when so many are on the move.

In Acts 17:21 Paul's audience was composed of both Athenian citizens (*politēs*) and "foreigners" or those just passing through Athens. (Many *xenoi* or tourists still visit Mars Hill.) Paul was invited to speak to them because he seemed to them to preach "foreign gods" alien to the Greek family of pagan deities. The thought of teachings "foreign" to Christianity is present in Hebrews 13:9.

A. T. Robertson notes that a *xenos* might be a host to strangers as well as a stranger. Hence in Romans 16:23 Paul calls Gaius his "guest friend" or host. He apparently was a man of means to have a house large enough to be "host" to the church in Rome.

One of the clearest uses of *xenos* is seen in Ephesians 2:12,

19. Here Paul sees the Gentiles as "aliens from the common-wealth of Israel, and strangers [xenoi] from the covenants of promise." But in Christ they are or may be "no more strangers [xenoi], and foreigners [paroikoi, resident aliens] but fellow-citizens [sumpolitai] with the saints, and of the household [oikeioi] of God." They are no longer those simply passing through the kingdom of God or "resident-aliens" of it. Instead they are kingdom-citizens, even residents in the house-hold of the King.

But while the Christian is a citizen in the colony of heaven (Phil. 3:20), he still bears a relationship to the world. Hebrews 11:13 sees this as a "foreigner" (xenos) just passing through or as a "foreigner" who takes up temporary residence (parepidēmos) on the earth. His citizenship and his home are elsewhere. This picture, of course, is drawn from the figure of Abraham and his seed traveling through a land but not becoming a part of it. But note that before being put in bondage the Israelites were "resident aliens" (paroikon) in Egypt (Acts 7:6). Moses enjoyed the same status in Midian (Acts 7:29).

But as a xenos in this world the Christian may expect to be treated as a xenos by the world. This thought is evident in I Peter 4:12. Speaking of persecution Peter says, "Beloved, think it not strange [xenizō, verb form] concerning the fiery trial which is to try you, as though some strange thing [xenos] happened unto you." To the Christian persecution or trouble may seem to be "foreign" to the Christian life. But it is to be expected by the very nature of a xenos. Jesus anticipated this in His warning to His disciples (John 15:18-19).

Because Christians are "resident aliens" (paroikous) and "temporary sojourners" (parepidēmous) in the world, they are urged to take no part in its "fleshly lusts" (I Peter 2:11).

So in these three words we see the picture of the relation-ship which the Christian bears to the world. He is a xenos, a foreigner just passing through. And although he may be a parepidēmos sojourning temporarily in the world, he is not to consider himself a part of its sinful life. As a paroikos he is a "resident alien" who is in the world to be busy about the business of his King. And while he may remain there for awhile, he is never to forget that he is a "fellow-citizen [fellow-citizens, *sumpolitoi*] with the "saints" in the Kingdom of God and a member "of the household [*oikeioi*] of God."